A Tempered Wind

Also by Karen Gershon

Poetry

The Relentless Year
Selected Poems
Legacies and Encounters
My Daughters, My Sisters
Coming Back from Babylon
Collected Poems

Nonfiction

We Came as Children
Postscript

Fiction

Burn Helen
The Bread of Exile
The Fifth Generation

A TEMPERED WIND

An Autobiography

KAREN GERSHON

Edited and with an introduction by Phyllis Lassner and Peter Lawson

NORTHWESTERN UNIVERSITY PRESS

Evanston, Illinois

Northwestern University Press
www.nupress.northwestern.edu

Printed in the United States of America

10 9 8 7 6 5 4 3 2 1

Library of Congress Cataloging-in-Publication Data

Gershon, Karen.

A tempered wind : an autobiography / Karen Gershon ; edited and with an introduction by Phyllis Lassner and Peter Lawson.

p. cm.

Includes bibliographical references.

ISBN 978-0-8101-2612-1 (cloth : alk. paper)—ISBN 978-0-8101-2613-8 (pbk.: alk. paper)

1. Gershon, Karen—Childhood and youth. 2. Jewish refugees—Great Britain—Personal narratives. 3. Jewish women authors—Great Britain—Biography. I. Lassner, Phyllis. II. Lawson, Peter, 1960– III. Title.
PR6057.E7Z46 2010
821.914—dc22

2009030681

∞ The paper used in this publication meets the minimum requirements of the American National Standard for Information Sciences—Permanence of Paper for Printed Library Materials, ANSI Z39.48-1992.

For the next generation of Lassners:
Julia, Brody, and Tyler

Contents

Introduction

Phyllis Lassner and Peter Lawson

Karen Gershon is best known in her adopted country of England as a poet and chronicler of the *Kindertransport* refugees, children who escaped Nazism in Germany, Austria, Poland, and Czechoslovakia from 1938 to 1939. The experience of losing both parents in the Holocaust while she was safe in Britain dominated Gershon's outlook. Many of her works are autobiographical, including this book, *A Tempered Wind* (1992). Recurrent themes in Gershon's poetry, novels, and autobiography are survivor's guilt, exile, and yearning for a lost home. Such yearning often finds expression in support for Israel as a home for the Jews, where she herself lived from 1968 to 1973.

Biographical Context

Gershon was born Kaethe Loewenthal on August 29, 1923, in Bielefeld, in the province of Westphalia, Germany. The family was middle-class; Gershon's father, Paul, was an architect, and her mother, Selma (née Schoenfeld), a housewife. There were three children: Anne, Kaethe, and Lise. When Hitler came to power in 1933, Kaethe was ten. Three years later, "Aryanization" at the local school led to her expulsion. As Jewish schools were established in response to legalized antisemitism, Kaethe entered, in 1937, a "non-Aryan" boarding school. The following year, she joined a Zionist program designed to select those best suited for immigration certificates to Mandatory Palestine. Both Kaethe and her sister Lise passed the course.

Gershon's self-portrait in *A Lesser Child: An Autobiography* (1994), which details this early period of her life, is the narrative precursor of *A Tempered Wind.* The earlier account is set in her childhood home of Bielefeld and portrays the impact of Nazism on a German Jewish child. To combat the undermining of their self-confidence by Nazi propaganda, Lise and Kaethe joined Maccabi Hatzair, a somewhat left-wing Zionist youth organization.[1]

Zionism gave the girls hope of normalization through escape from "their otherness" in Germany.[2] Kaethe freely acknowledges that "to be like everyone else was what she wanted; she was willing to go to Palestine to achieve it."[3] "They had been preparing themselves for years and now prepared their luggage to go to the Land of Israel."[4] However, after *Kristallnacht,* November 9 to 10, 1938, "the worst day for Jews in Germany since the Middle Ages," Lise and Kaethe were put on a *Kindertransport* for England.[5] This earlier volume of Gershon's autobiography ends at the Bielefeld train station, where the girls see their parents for the last time. They arrived in Harwich, Essex, on December 15, 1938.

A Tempered Wind continues the personal history begun in *A Lesser Child.* Chronologically, it starts in December 1938, when both Loewenthal girls arrive at Dovercourt reception camp, in England, though the narrative begins in July 1943 and relates the tragic death of Gershon's twenty-two-year-old sister Anne "from purpura, an extremely rare condition which meant that her blood had lost its capacity to clot." The children's travels progress as they are sent to Scotland in February 1939, staying in the stately home of the Balfour family. This seems auspicious, in light of the 1917 Balfour Declaration, which promised Jews a national home in Palestine. Indeed, the seventeen-year-old Lise leaves for Mandatory Palestine before war breaks out, but Kaethe is too young for a permit and cannot join her. By the time the British government makes fresh entry permits available in June and July 1940, "the idea of our leaving England just then had been abandoned."

The unsettled nature of refugee life had effects at the most intimate level. For example, it was homesickness that spurred Gershon's marriage to a distant cousin, Walter, in 1942. "He is my Bielefeld," she writes. "It doesn't seem fair to him, that I married him because of this instead of for himself." It comes as no surprise, therefore, when they separate the following year. In 1944, Kaethe takes a scholarship examination to read French at Edinburgh University. Interestingly, she chooses to be examined in the arcane area of "Medieval English History." Gershon explains: "I knew more about modern European history but felt that I could not cope, emotionally, with the period which included the First World War, in which my father had fought beside those who were now his enemies against those who had saved me from the concentration camps."

Having passed the examination and begun her degree, Gershon experiences a change of heart. She decides that a degree "was altogether irrelevant to what I wanted to do with this life which my parents and the British people had preserved for me," and leaves after only one term. This decision follows soon after she discovers from the Red Cross that her parents have not survived the concentration camps: "Late in April [1946 . . .] the Red Cross had published lists of the names of those who had survived the concentration camps." "I found the list headed Westfalen (Westphalia); it consisted of only one page. I looked down it; there was not even a name beginning with *L.*" Kaethe discovers more about her parents' deaths from Walter:

> I have forgotten just when Walter, with the British Army, passed through Bielefeld; it must have been sometime in May. He spoke with Jewish survivors who had been deported together with my parents to the Riga ghetto in December 1941. He was told that the Jews worked there as slaves for the *Wehrmacht* and that my father, after a year or so, was one morning found dead in his bed—he had a weak heart—and that my mother was known to have survived until the autumn of 1944, when the Germans put an end to the ghetto. No one could tell him what had happened to her.

The autobiography ends with Gershon's resolution "to begin another family—which I did—and to write—which I continue to do."

Historical Context

Among all the memorials, narratives, and expressions of national consciousness of the Holocaust, Britain's may be like no other. Despite its acclaimed Holocaust exhibition and wartime heroism, among all those people and places producing Holocaust literature and art, Britain has probably received the least attention. While it is true that there are fewer survivors, testimony projects, and Holocaust exhibitions in Britain than elsewhere, its writing is powerful and significant. And yet, even the most recent American anthologies and surveys of Holocaust writing omit the contributions of British memoirists and imaginative writers of the Holocaust and its aftermath. One reason may be that until fairly recently, those who escaped to Britain have not been considered among those we identify as Holocaust survivors. Neither the refugees who came as individuals or families nor those participating in the *Kindertransport* suffered the ghettos or camps. They are not among the children who were hidden with non-Jewish families or in convents, and they did not pass on the "Aryan" side with forged identity papers. They escaped the Holocaust before the roundups and deportations began.

As this newly available *Kindertransport* memoir attests, however, those who were saved by Britain did not escape the effects of the Holocaust. Most lost their immediate and extended families, and, as Jewish refugees in a nation desiring unity at the moment of its greatest threat, their experience of safe haven was often compromised by their being considered enemy aliens or unassimilable. Now, so many decades later, a body of literature is emerging that gives us firsthand access to their story. In addition to the external, social, and political opprobrium felt by the refugees, a powerful element in their new world was the tension they felt between veneration for those who had experienced the Holocaust and their own displacement. Although this literature makes no claim to represent any events within the world of Holocaust atrocities, it occupies a telling space between that world and the one that became the refugees' safe harbor. The losses of family and of personal and cultural identities left an emotional void that refugee writers like Karen Gershon transform into an imaginative space. They fill this emptiness with portraits of remembered people and places as they imagine them so many decades later. Marita Grimwood asserts that "it is the very absence of [the Holocaust] experience that is often an uncanny presence" in the writing of the Second Generation.[6] Refugee writers in Britain create an "uncanny presence" by fusing memory and imagination in writing that cannot recapture their lost people and places. Families, friends, and communities are there and not there, alive in memory and imagined reconstruction or even in fantasies and allegorical fairy tales, but always disappearing once again in the folds of new realities.

The complications of the World War II refugee experience in Britain have produced a literature that adds significantly to our knowledge of the Holocaust as an event and as an effect. *A Tempered Wind* reveals a relationship that complicates the story of heroic rescue by the British. It highlights the urgency of debates about relationships between the cultural identities and historical memory of both the rescuer nation and the rescued. As the unfolding narrative tells us, despite a vaunted tradition of tolerance, British wartime fears about fifth columns and economic austerity contributed to the unease with which European Jews were received on British soil. Not only could the Jewish refugees not share the nation's historical consciousness and its traditions, but everything about Jews' differences made them seem foreign and often suspect. On the other hand, so many refugees were treated kindly by individual host families and those Jewish and non-Jewish organizations responsible for their rescue. In turn, Jewish refugees were infinitely grateful for a safe haven, and many became eager to acculturate.

In 1938 and 1939, between *Kristallnacht* and the onset of war, the British government, with help from Jewish and Quaker organizations, rescued around ten thousand Jewish and "non-Aryan" children from Germany, Austria, Poland, and Czechoslovakia.[7]

Commemorated in seventieth-anniversary exhibitions around Britain, this rescue continues to represent an uplifting reminder of the nation's moral rectitude in the face of Europe's capitulations.[8] In terms of its modern historical narrative, the story of a singularly humanitarian Britain has been especially important to the nation's (and former empire's) sense of itself, as we can see in a parliamentary statement of that time. In 1933, when German Jews were already caught in the Nazis' tightening vise, Commander Oliver Locker-Lampson, MP, introduced a bill on July 26 creating citizenship opportunities "in Palestine for Jews deprived of citizenship elsewhere," reminding the house "that it is un-English, it is caddish to bully a minority," and suggested that the British Empire should "stand by Jewry in its trouble."[9] While there is no doubt that the British deserve unequivocal recognition for the *Kindertransport* and other rescues, Karen Gershon's memoir and her fiction attest to the traumatic effects of losing their homes and families, of adaptation and acculturation, that should be considered for a full understanding of Britain's historical identity.

The children's experiences of loss, cultural disorientation, and uncertainty about the future produced a sense of dislocation that could not be resolved by the ambiguous security Britain provided. Instead, what may have been most consistent in the experience of rescue was a continuous disjunction between memories of a stable self that were now unsustainable and an insecure selfhood in the present. Most Jewish refugees eventually adapted and went on to live highly productive lives, but as so many have recounted, the emotional road to success and stability was chiseled out of feelings of abandonment and self-doubt. If we consider that the transported children were between three and sixteen years old, then the experience of being wrenched away from their parents combines both the normative psychic jolt of developmental separation and the disturbing historical fact that most would never see their parents again. Their extenuating circumstance was that loss of family was absolute; there was to be no psychological and social process of renegotiating parent-child relations as these children grew to adulthood and individuation. Regardless of whether it would have been psychologically possible, no emotional compensation was available in the experience of searching for emotional attachment, consolation, and relationship in the children's foster families or group homes.

Despite the best intentions of host families and groups, because the rescue was predicated on a temporary stay and because of cultural mismatches and misunderstandings, the establishment of emotionally intimate and secure relations was rare. In order to feel accepted by their foster parents, the children had to abandon cultural norms and social conventions that had been ingrained as a result of their various degrees and types of Jewish observances and identities. For the more reflective and older children, including Gershon, who was fifteen when she was transported, this meant a conscious and difficult choice, for they learned that they had to be grateful to those who sheltered them while abandoning much of what they held dear. On the other hand, as Andrea Hammel points out, it was generally assumed at the time that most of the children were "too young to remember any trauma or, at least, it was considered easier for them to integrate into a new society."[10] By the time the war ended and the facts about most parents' deaths in the camps and ghettos emerged, it was too late to express feelings of abandonment related to the lost parents. There were those, however, who would harbor such feelings without resolution. Furthermore, unlike survivors who had experienced the Holocaust's tortures directly, there seemed to be no targets toward which their emotionally logical responses of outrage and hatred could be aimed. As they were told and internalized, they had grown up in the six years of rescue and were already embarked on building new lives as

Britons. They were counseled to move on, and so, in effect, were silenced in both thought and speech.

The story of Britain's rescue of the Jews is strained by the responses of both British officials and the Jewish community. Colonial injunctions prevented endangered Jews from entering Palestine and other colonies, and domestic restrictions kept most parents from joining their children in Britain.[11] Even as Jewish refugees were adapting economically and culturally, the Jewish community, complying with official expectations, insisted that the refugees remake themselves in a British image by revising their European Jewish identities and styles. The transformation proved not to be easy, however. Social welfare agencies issued booklets with lists of dos and don'ts for acquiring British manners, but not necessarily citizenship. Anglo-Jewry's responses to Jewish refugees were driven by official British ambivalence and a history of antisemitism. Despite cooperation between the Jewish and non-Jewish communities on behalf of child refugees, apprehension about reigniting antisemitism by its own activism prevailed in the Jewish community.[12] This anxiety is apparent in the cautious instructions issued by the Jewish community to Jewish immigrants, which mirrored British attitudes, as in a booklet produced by the German Jewish Aid Committee in conjunction with the Jewish Board of Deputies, *While You Are in England: Helpful Information and Guidance for Every Refugee.* As the following proviso indicates, the agency's urge to be "helpful" is matched by broader impulses to keep the refugees in their designated place as forever alienated but grateful:

> Do not criticize any government regulations, nor the way things are done over here. Do not speak of "how much better this or that is done in Germany." It may be true in some matters, but it weighs as nothing against the sympathy and freedom and liberty of England which are now given to you. Never forget that point.[13]

This final edict carried the message that, although integration was not expected of the refugees, acculturation, loyalty, and gratitude were. Considering that the pamphlet was prepared by a Jewish organization, its voice may strike us as perplexing. Instead of the empathy or support we could assume of a community organization addressing its beleaguered exiled brethren, we hear paternalistic injunctions. This voice does not, however, originate without a context. A complicating factor was the not quite perfect fit of Anglo-Jewry and British cultural style and values. Unlike the general populace, which, despite class clashes, felt unified in its resolve to defend itself against a common enemy, Anglo-Jewry had to expend "scarce resources and time to combating antisemitism in Britain during the war" while worrying about the refugees as well as those left behind, not to mention their own fate should Hitler invade Britain.[14] A positive message conveyed to refugees by the government and the Anglo-Jewish community, however, was that the children of the *Kindertransport* would be treated to all the political and cultural benefits of a humane society. British schools and homes would educate and acculturate them. The system would embrace them.

Yet, instead of being invited to join the battle of the British Empire against the Third Reich, adult refugees were viewed with mistrust as itinerants, as lacking a nativist loyalty, and as a burden on national security and the economy. Boys and girls of sixteen and older were in danger of being interned, and many boys were included with those men deported to Canada and Australia as enemy aliens once France had fallen and the British began to fear a German invasion. One of Karen Gershon's interview subjects in her collective autobiography of refugees, *We Came as Children,* remembers the perplexity of being rescued and then interned:

> To be told that the country of my birth was the declared enemy of the country of my adoption was hardly conducive to the settling-down process. . . . I learned very quickly to omit any reference to my nationality when being introduced to people, and I adopted the same attitude to my religion. At this time I wanted

> above all to be "accepted" and that meant pretending to be as average and English as possible.[15]

The presence of foreign Jews and their history of estrangement also created a disturbance in Britain's narrative of national continuity and identity. A social survey of October 1940 revealed that of "all comments concerning oppressed people, 47 percent were directed towards the Jews, yet only 18 percent felt Jews were deserving sympathy."[16] Having escaped their toxic fate as despised and feared objects of the Third Reich, refugees were now suspicious objects of British benevolence. For example, like Gershon, many of the refugee children had come from upper middle-class homes, where higher education and professional occupations had been the norm. Whatever transition into British society they might have expected was dashed, however, by their newly acquired status. One contributor to Gershon's collective autobiography reports, "When I came to England I thought that now I would be like everyone else, that my life would be normal. When asked what I wanted to be I said a doctor. The woman who was filling the form in said: 'I can't put that down—you must remember that you are a refugee.'"[17] Though there were many instances of nurture and support among Jewish and non-Jewish host families, and some children qualified for higher education scholarships, this unsettling response contributed to the refugees' feeling that their Jewish identity was being denied. There were too many signs in the Jewish and non-Jewish communities of the class-bound and Anglo-Christian character of the nation.

In addition, the government exploited the anxieties of the Jewish community with the reminder that a sizable Jewish immigration could lead to an antisemitic backlash. Instead of being integrated into Britain's major Jewish communities, those who were not interned and those who were later released were dispersed around the country and instructed "to keep a low profile, so as to avoid the impression of a substantial and menacing Jewish body within England."[18] While dependent and therefore entwined with the host nation, the Jews were, by their differences, severed from Britain's cultural traditions. Although it was generous toward the refugees, the Anglo-Jewish community did little to bridge this chasm; indeed, its insecurities produced responses that were more puzzling and disturbing than helpful.

Although Anglo-Jews took pride in the distinctive aspects of their religious identity and practices, they expressed them almost apologetically. Despite the increasing material successes of the Jewish communities, their manners and codes of respectability had developed and remained in the shadows of antisemitism. For those Jewish refugees who stayed on after the war, becoming British meant assimilating to British culture but submerging their own history and culture under the weightier if tremulous traditions of Anglo-Jewry. So often, especially for children and adolescent refugees, the curriculum for learning Anglo-Jewish social codes included abandoning the past responsible for shaping them. Refugee Hans Schneider testifies:

> A past in a different country is a burden on a teenager attempting to make a new life for himself or herself, and it leads to (I am tempted to say "requires") memory loss of one's previous life. Silence, unless with others similarly placed, is needed by a young outsider for fitting into a [homogeneous] society—a silence which becomes deeply ingrained.[19]

Many of the ten thousand children saved by Britain were driven to write their memoirs when their fiftieth reunion confronted them with the passage of time, receding memories, and their shared sense of a prevailing silence about their refugee experiences.

As Gershon reveals, the children also had to face disjunctions between mostly ordinary middle-class childhoods and the uncertainties and losses brought about by emigration and growing up without family. Writing decades later from an inquiring perspective on events and relationships they hardly and rarely understood as children, many writers who had experienced the *Kindertransport* sought a narrative form that would suggest the discontinuities and incoherencies of their experiences. These writers also questioned whether a narrative about such a dramatic rupture between past and present could only be coherent if it is unified by its fragments of social and emotional realities.

Even when these memoirs follow a chronological structure, scenes from a past overshadowed by belated knowledge suggest fable more than realistic form. What the characters don't understand guides the narrative rather than the pathway to knowledge and adult experience. Like those writers who experienced the immediacy of the Holocaust, these authors turned to references to other genres. In Gershon's case, as in her *Kindertransport* novel, *Bread of Exile* (1985), literary allusions to works such as *Jane Eyre* provide the template through which to narrate the jagged process of growing up. Instead of subscribing to the coming-of-age model of the bildungsroman to show how they face adult disillusionments, these writers offer a critique by turning such literary expectations upside down.

Gershon's memoir gives expression to the terror of familial rupture and abandonment, the fear and reality of the Nazi danger, as well as the encoded double messages about British integration. The detail with which she recounts her experience provides a picture of historical and psychological realities that have only recently been given the attention they deserve. Her story offers us an emotionally complicated and compelling portrayal that is not meant to comfort. Instead, it addresses our desire for reconciliation, resolution, and recovery by frustrating it. With often searing candor, she challenges such desire with fresh insights into the lingering effects of the traumas provoked by the refugees' experience of rupture. Instead of comforting us with participation in a character's understanding, Gershon's memoir forces readers to see the necessary failure of Holocaust stories to do so.

A Tempered Wind

There are several themes woven through the tapestry of refugee experience presented in *A Tempered Wind:* home and exile, Jewish and female otherness, writing and the making of a writer. Significantly, *A Tempered Wind* exists on a continuum with the majority of Gershon's oeuvre in being autobiographical. In this, it resembles her poetry, novels, and, one might say, sociological studies.

Gershon's *Selected Poems* and *We Came as Children* were published in 1966; and while the one focused on personal autobiographical material (after the manner of the contemporaneous confessional poets, such as Sylvia Plath and Anne Sexton), the other offered a collective autobiography of the *Kindertransport* generation. Of the ten thousand children sent to Britain, two hundred and thirty-four contributed to *We Came as Children.* Gershon assembled their recollections without attribution, thus foregrounding the shared social experience of these exiled Jewish children. She also divided the book into sociological sections, with titles such as "The Reception Camps" and "Institutions." In a description of what is clearly her own return to Bielefeld in 1963, Gershon writes: "My Jewish childhood in Nazi Germany and my orphan exile at the age of fifteen must remain a part of my life always."[20] Elsewhere she states: "It has taken me twenty-five years to learn to accept what I am: a German Jew."[21] Several critics praised *We Came as Children* as, for example, an "overwhelming book."[22] There was similar praise for the *Selected Poems,* for which Gershon won a British Arts Council Poetry Award in 1967.

What becomes clear throughout Gershon's oeuvre is that her sense of "home" is always provisional. As she writes in the poem "Married Love" (1975): "I sought a home it would not hurt to lose / Which would outweigh for me the one I lost."[23] Whatever home Gershon's autobiographical characters find, they remain continuously aware of their exilic condition. It is no coincidence that her heavily autobiographical novel is titled *The Bread of Exile.* As one critic notes, "the heroine of her tale, thirteen-year-old Inge, travelled a similar route" to Gershon's own *Kindertransport* journey.[24] The familiar autobiographical figure of a *Kindertransport* orphan reappears in a later novel, *The Fifth Generation* (1987). Ron Baker astutely comments that "Gershon's sensitivity to the central character's problems is of a special kind, drawing perhaps from some of her own experiences as a refugee."[25] Similarly, Gershon's novel *Burn Helen* (1980) depicts home as provisional. Helen is a gentile orphan who "had always believed that she thought, compulsively, I wish I were dead, because she felt guilty about having survived her family"[26] In effect, Helen is suffering a species of Holocaust survivor's guilt. Like Gershon, she is an orphan of World War II: "*They were killed in the blitz. Her whole family was.*"[27] Committed to domesticity as a wife and mother, Helen nonetheless feels exiled and estranged from her new family since "there was nothing inevitable about being related to [her husband] Paul."[28] In her experience, Helen resembles many of the contributors to *We Came as Children.*

Home is a major theme of *A Tempered Wind.* Feeling homesick, Kaethe seeks whatever means at her disposal to have familiar things around her. As a refugee classified as such with other "aliens," she writes of her attempts to belong somewhere. For example, at Dovercourt reception camp Gershon tries to turn the surrounding "strangeness into home" by lighting the Sabbath candles, "one of the few observances which Jewish ritual allocates to girls and women; it was the sole action available there by which any girl could have domesticated the reception camp." It seems that the religious gesture has less significance than the creation of a provisionally safe space. Indeed, as Gershon writes, "Lise and I attended the Friday night service, less because we believed in God—though we did—than because we knew that in its ritual we would feel at home."

When Gershon expects to feel at home, for example among English Jews, she is often left disappointed:

> On Friday night (my second in Leeds) I went to the synagogue, not to pray but just so as to feel at home among Jews. All the melodies were different, so that I couldn't join in the singing, and it was worse feeling an outsider because I hadn't expected it. . . . The women sat separately; they all looked at me, but no one spoke to me or invited me home, as Jews are supposed to do with strangers.

At the end of the evening, Gershon remains an outsider. Apparently, British Jews behave as coldly as British gentiles toward refugees. Gershon grows accustomed to "the lack of understanding . . . from the British," together with their "icy smile to cool my feelings." Such alienation spurs her Zionism: "This wish, this need to be at home where I lived, that was the essence of my Zionism." It also encourages her to write, because "having the incentive to be writing, writing, I almost stopped feeling homesick." Indeed, Gershon's Zionism and writing appear closely connected in *A Tempered Wind*. Her career as a writer begins with "stories, and essays, and poems, and a whole sequence of 'Letters from Jerusalem'; in my imagination I lived there." Both writing and an imagined homeland (Jerusalem) offer the young Gershon escape from the alienation of her refugee experience.

Such alienation relates to gender as well as Jewishness, sexism as well as antisemitism. Gershon depicts the twenty-year-old Kaethe as a "small, pale, sad-eyed, tongue-tied girl in bright clothing, a maverick among Jews as well as non-Jews, in England." Her difference is gender-based: a "girl in bright clothing" amid the "dark coats" of Jewish men. Kaethe appears as a vulnerable "girl," though in fact she is a young woman. Indeed, physically and psychologically Kaethe has "stopped growing" since she left her mother. As her separation "was meant to be temporary but was permanent," Kaethe's "feelings for her [mother], against her, remained frozen at that [adolescent] stage." It is therefore no coincidence that, even when married, "with her hair loose about her shoulders, no make-up, and in her simple clothes, she looks like a schoolgirl." With this vulnerability, there is "the additional discrimination against females" to face. This is why Gershon decides not to take the entrance exam for Oxford or Cambridge. In England (more so than in Scotland, where the narrative closes), there is hostility toward Gershon as a Jew, a German, a refugee, and a woman.

Conclusion

Assimilating to her English environment, Kaethe anglicized her name to Karen and, in 1957, adopted the pen name Gershon. Gershon had been her father's Hebrew name, meaning "stranger in a strange land." In a Zionist attempt to cease being "Gershon," and to feel at home, she moved to Israel for several years, but returned to England in late 1973. In her foreword to the 1989 edition of *We Came as Children,* Gershon confronts the tensions of her situation as a Jew in England and her reasons for not remaining in Israel:

> When I came to this country I was on my way to what was then called Palestine. While working on this book I realised that, for me, England would always remain a foster-home. I then continued my journey, together with the family I had made. Perhaps I had left it too late.
>
> I feel more at home in Israel than I do in England, but I don't feel at home there either, and that is worse, because there I still expect to be able to feel at home. Here I am reconciled.[29]

Clearly, Gershon felt truly at home neither in Israel nor in England; claiming to be reconciled to life outside Israel, she implies a coming to terms with being a Jew in the Diaspora.

Gershon was among the first of the *Kindertransport* generation who wrote in order to confront the experiences of Nazism. The critic C. B. Cox is not alone in claiming that Gershon is one of the "major war poets" of 1939 to 1945.[30] She is also, we believe, a major prose writer. There are deep silences in Gershon's understated composition, corresponding to loss, absence, and unspeakable grief. As she writes in her poem "Mine Is the Bat's Scream": "I'm not as silent as you think: / mine is the bat's scream you can't hear."[31] There is also a unique style of German English Gershon crafted to convey her foreignness both to England and to standard English; she writes in *A Tempered Wind,* for example, "My parents were by whom I wanted to be looked after, my sisters were with whom I wanted to share"; "I asked myself, this is for what I have given up going to Wales with Pummi?"; "I had already begun to make poems in English."

Gershon's poetry and collective autobiography of the *Kindertransport, We Came as Children,* have been widely admired, while her personal autobiographies have not, so far, received the recognition they deserve. It is hoped that this publication of *A Tempered Wind* will extend literary pleasure and serious interest in Gershon's autobiographical oeuvre.

Notes

1. Karen Gershon, *A Lesser Child: An Autobiography* (London: Peter Owen, 1994), 81.
2. Ibid., 115.
3. Ibid., 116.
4. Ibid., 190.
5. Ibid., 187.
6. Marita Grimwood, *Holocaust Literature of the Second Generation* (New York: Palgrave, 2007), 3.
7. The *Kindertransport* was organized by the World Movement for the Care of Children, which brought 9,354 children to Britain, including 7,482 who were Jewish. This figure represents less than 1 percent of the children killed in the Holocaust. Priority was given to orphans, children

from single-parent homes, those whose parents were in concentration camps, and boys targeted for incarceration. Each child was permitted one suitcase and ten reichsmarks.

8. Denmark and Bulgaria, which rescued their Jews, were exceptions. Records show that resistance to rescue includes North America, for after debates in Congress and in state legislatures, after complaints that refugee children would take over the jobs of American citizens, the United States decided against any such rescue. For all its vast emptiness, Canada took in a total of five thousand Jews. Tony Kushner notes that in the period 1938 to 1939, "more than 40 percent of the Jews who escaped the Nazis found refuge in Britain," albeit on temporary visas (*The Holocaust and the Liberal Imagination* [Oxford: Blackwell, 1994], 51). The history of British refugee policies begins with the Aliens Act of 1905, which, with further restrictions implemented before and after World War I, limited Jewish immigration from eastern Europe. From 1933 to 1938, the British government tried to effect policies that would balance self-interest with its desire to appear humane. The result was to admit those who brought wealth or scientific, artistic, or technological talents, albeit against the protests of professional organizations. By 1938, visas were being granted to those who were economically self-sufficient or had British guarantors. Jewish women were admitted on domestic service visas. The *Kindertransport* was made possible by refugee agencies' guaranteeing fifty pounds sterling for each child to be paid against their subsequent reemigration. For details, see David Cesarani's introduction in Mark Jonathan and Deborah Oppenheimer, *Into the Arms of Strangers: Stories of the Kindertransport* (London: Bloomsbury, 2000).

9. Quoted in A. J. Sherman, *Island Refuge: Britain and Refugees from the Third Reich, 1933–1939* (London: Frank Cass, 1994), 39.

10. Andrea Hammel, "Between Adult Narrator and Narrated Child," *Holocaust Studies* 11, no. 2 (Autumn 2005): 65–66.

11. The Colonial Office claimed that the colonies, including Kenya, Tanganyika, and Northern Rhodesia, couldn't "make a serious contribution to the problem" (Sherman, *Island Refuge,* 103).

12. Colin Holmes makes the point that, despite British differences, "a tradition of anti-semitism in Britain" was not "insignificant" and to dismiss it as such would be "a cruel deception" (*Anti-Semitism in British Society, 1876–1939* [London: Edward Arnold, 1979], 234).

13. The German Jewish Aid Committee, in conjunction with the Jewish Board of Deputies, *While You Are in England: Helpful Information and Guidance for Every Refugee* (London: Woburn House, n.d.), 12.

14. Kushner, *Holocaust,* 131.

15. Karen Gershon, ed., *We Came as Children: A Collective Autobiography* (1966; repr., London: Gollancz, 1989), 89.

16. Tony Kushner, *The Persistence of Prejudice: Antisemitism in British Society During the Second World War* (Manchester, U.K.: Manchester University Press, 1989), 117.

17. Gershon, *We Came as Children,* 40.

18. Richard Bolchover, *British Jewry and the Holocaust* (Cambridge: Cambridge University Press, 1993), 50.

19. Hans Schneider, review of Jonathan and Oppenheimer, *Into the Arms of Strangers, Shofar* 20, no. 4 (Summer 2002), 116.

20. Gershon, *We Came as Children,* 159.

21. Ibid., 149.

22. Raymond Mortimer, "We Came as Children," *Sunday Times* (London), May 15, 1966. See also Lena Jeger, "Body, Soul, and Passport," *Guardian* (London), May 13, 1966; and Julia Neuberger, "A Growing Disquiet," *Observer* (London), March 11, 1990.

23. Karen Gershon, *Collected Poems* (London: Macmillan, 1990), 100–101.

24. Meir Perloff, "Two Heroines," *Jewish Chronicle* (London), May 10, 1985.

25. Ron Baker, "German-Jewish Confusions," *Jewish Chronicle* (London), April 10, 1987.

26. Karen Gershon, *Burn Helen* (Brighton, U.K.: Harvester Press, 1980), 77.

27. Ibid., 2.

28. Ibid., 86.

29. Gershon, *We Came as Children,* 9.

30. C. B. Cox, "Selected Poems," *Spectator* (London), August 5, 1966, 180.

31. Karen Gershon, *Grace Notes* (Toppesfield, U.K.: Happy Dragons' Press, 2002), 18.

A Tempered Wind

For my family: past, present, future

God tempers the wind . . . to the shorn lamb.

—Laurence Sterne

ANNE'S DEATH

July–August 1943

(Mainly Bristol)

My mother, speaking of our emigration, used to say, "At least I want you to remain together." And so the three of us came to England, Lise aged sixteen and I a year younger; but Anne at seventeen was too old for the scheme rescuing children and we were never to be all three together again.

Anne came in the spring of 1939, going her own way in exile as she had done at home. If, during the almost four and a half years she lived in England, she sought me out more than twice I have forgotten it. I must have known at the time but do not remember knowing that Lise, on her way to what was then called Palestine, passed through London, and she and Anne were together then, for two or even three days. Anne was living in a hostel with other refugees waiting for a place on a Zionist training farm. She had put on weight, Lise told me many years later, from living on cheap food. Expecting Lise, she had for days eaten hardly at all, thus saving her allowance in order to be able to take Lise about, show her the sights of London, treat her to a meal. To know and imagine them having been together without me is, even after more than half a century, so unacceptable to me, emotionally, that though I remember Lise recently describing the dress which Anne passed on to her on that occasion, I can't remember what she said about it. When we were children at home it was always I who inherited Anne's dresses.

Of course Anne and I exchanged letters, but this meant little more than that I knew where she was. She did not tell me anything of importance about her life, had always thought me either too little or too inadequate for confidences. I did not try to make her be of help to me for fear of making her see me as a burden.

Anne was on the David Eder farm in Kent when, in May 1940, German nationals, in those parts girls as well as boys, were being interned; she was sent to the Isle of Man.

"I am making allowances for Mr. Churchill," she wrote to me, showing more understanding than the government. Her internment did not shake my belief that she was in charge of her life.

As far as I was concerned, it meant that, through Anne, I could continue to exchange letters with my parents. At least once, they sent her a parcel, including a bar of Lindt chocolate and a packet of Leibnitz-Keks, her favourite biscuits: she sent me the wrappers as my share of their present. Not a token share only, because their familiarity meant something to us and they were the part that would keep. The biscuit wrapper was overprinted with the demand for a certain number (six?) of bread coupons. Perhaps the Nazis had spread the rumour that the interned Germans were starving? If so, did it mean, she asked my opinion, that our parents believed this? Or were they trying to reassure us that they still got enough to eat? At least it showed that they had ration cards, which some people said Jews hadn't.

I had witnessed, experienced, almost six years of ever-increasing discrimination against the Jews, but I did not allow myself to realise that things were bound to continue to get worse for them. I could not bear to think of our parents' life without us. I preferred not to think about them, pretending to myself that this was because I lacked the necessary information for my thoughts to coincide with reality and that therefore my thinking about them amounted to self-deception.

I wrote to Anne, "Surely Mutti and Papa sent you those

things because they love you," which was what I, in her place, would have wanted to hear. And most likely the truth.

She wrote that she would not consider joining the Forces until there was a Jewish Brigade. Later, she wrote that she would join the Forces once foreigners serving in them were no longer discriminated against. She gave up that condition, too. She joined the ATS [Auxiliary Territorial Service] in the summer of 1941.

When she came to visit me in Leeds, that was her first leave: genuinely the first opportunity either of us had to seek the other out. She was then twenty and we had not been together for almost three years. We were not much together then: I was a domestic servant living in, and she spent most of her time with Stan, a private in the Pioneer Corps, also on leave; they had been together on *hachsharah* (meaning preparation, i.e., for kibbutz life) and fallen in love. He was a Pole, with a wife and child still in Warsaw. Because he mattered to Anne, I tried to like him but couldn't. They gave me the feeling—no: I had the feeling when I was with them both that they grudged me the time and would rather have been by themselves.

If I saw Anne alone more than once I have forgotten it. She came to the house on Yom Kippur, while my master and mistress were attending the synagogue. We sat in the kitchen together. She said that she wasn't fasting and was hungry, and I cut her some bread, and put out my jar of jam and what was left of my week's butter ration. I watched her eating and was happy to be able to do something for her, happy that she allowed me to be of use to her. At breakfast time the next morning my mistress scolded me for having finished my butter ration and not having much jam left either. It made me feel euphoric, because Anne was the cause of it.

In July 1943, Anne came to visit me in Edinburgh. By then I was married, and as a soldier's wife I was expected to take time off only when my husband was on leave. And though I would rather have spent time with Anne even if I had still loved

Walter—it was Anne who was the love of my life—I lacked the self-confidence to defy the conventions. She was to arrive, from I think it was Ilfracombe, early in the morning and I had arranged to come in to work late.

I had misunderstood her instructions. While I was waiting for her in my room, she remained at the station, and when I didn't come eventually made her way to my place of work. Where I eventually went, not knowing what else to do.

As I turned into George Street I saw her coming towards me. That I had not expected to see her there caused my feelings to respond as if I had been expecting not to see her at all: for the past two hours I had been telling myself that she must have changed her mind and found a more worthwhile way of spending her leave than coming to see me.

I did not know what to do with the emotion which the sight of her generated. From when I had been too little to keep my hands clean and to take care she had schooled me not to touch her and not to kiss her without permission, and then it had to be done in accordance with her instructions. Now we merely shook hands, neither of us wanting to be, in the street, more demonstrative than the British.

And instantly quarreled. Why had I not been at the station? She had not told me at which one she would be arriving: there were two. But I had known which train she would be taking; I should have enquired.

I was appalled to have given her cause at once to find fault with me. I cursed myself for having forfeited two possible hours of her company—considering every moment of it as precious as if I had known that within a month she would be dead.

She had left her bag at my employer's office. She had drunk a glass of sherry with him. He was to ask me her rank, having mistaken her for an officer: such were her appearance and her behaviour. When he saw us together he told me to take the rest of the morning off.

When I mentioned her coming to my landlady, she had told me that Anne could sleep in the attic, which she herself had been occupying: she had already decided to move into the kitchen so as to have an additional room to let. It did not seem right to me that I should have a better room, a better bed than Anne, who had conditioned me to think that, for her, even the best was barely good enough. I suggested that we should change places, but she would not consider it. Walter would be getting a weekend pass and she said that I owed it to him to keep the double bed.

"Apart from Saturday night, then," I suggested. But she was adamant, and it vexed me that I needed to choose between continuing to argue and letting her sleep in the attic. I showed it to her and she said, "I've slept in worse places." That made it even more important to me that she should have my room: I wanted to do something for her. "This is fine for me," she said, upsetting me further with this evidence of how much refugee life had changed her.

I ought to have known it: at home, she had refused to dirty her hands even with a duster and now she was a medical orderly.

It was summer but perhaps the weather was bad: I think of her as exchanging warmth for cold when she left my comfortable room—or perhaps what I'm thinking of is the comfort of our being together. That evening, when she was tired, she said—quite as in the old days—that *I* needed to go to bed because I had to get up in the morning to go to work. And she said, "I have varicose veins, like Mutti. I'll show you if you come up, just give me time enough to get undressed."

Nothing else that had happened or that she had said so far so reinstated me as her little sister: how was I to know how long was time enough, not for me but for her? My diffidence about being able to please her counterbalanced that I was more at home in the flat, in the town where we happened to be, that I was already married, that in my opinion I was more in charge of my life than she was of hers, being a soldier.

Lise and I had never been allowed to see her—as we did each other—undressing or even naked; Anne and everything about her was as if sacred ground to me. It did not occur to me at the time, when I saw her sitting on the edge of my landlady's bed with bare legs, that the rest of her flesh was covered up because it also bore bruises and she could not expect even me to agree with her that these were all varicose veins. Which were nothing to fear because they were familiar to us from the sight of our mother's legs.

The bruises on Anne's legs did not look the same. It surprised me that Anne should think they did: I was used to her knowing better than I. I said so.

Some weeks before, I was later told, when she, among others, had been asked to give blood, she had refused, saying that she was anaemic. Her friends had laughed at her, she looked in such good health; they may have thought, as I would have done, that she abhorred the idea of such sharing. No, I would have thought that she considered her blood too precious: I would have considered it so. I can tell only how I saw her and not how she was.

If she was frightened by the bruising she did not allow me to know it. I was not frightened by it; I no longer believed in God but I still had faith in the benevolence of life. I had faith in Anne: if there was something wrong with her health—and, obviously, there was—she would know how to have it put right.

She told me, "I've had my period for the past six weeks." I was too ignorant to see the connection; I was pleased that she was confiding in me as if we were equals.

The doctor I was registered with happened to be a woman. The next morning, while I was at work, Anne went to see her.

If, throughout her stay, she was worried about her health, she did not allow me to know it. On the last evening of her leave, she dawdled over saying good-night and eventually suggested that instead of going upstairs she should share my bed. Perhaps this is what makes me remember those days as cold enough for me to have lit the fire; there was no way of heating the attic. I could not believe that she, who always meant what she said, meant it this time: I knew her to be fastidious. We could exchange beds, I suggested, did she want me to exchange the bedding?

What she wanted was my company.

All the rest of my memories of our penultimate time together have been swallowed up by what happened afterwards.

Instead of returning to her unit, at the end of her leave she reported to the castle, which served as a military hospital. She was sent to the Southmead Hospital in Bristol, at that time the centre for blood diseases. From there, she wrote to me, a page and a half on small paper, telling me among other things that on the Thursday she would be having "a small operation."

It did not worry me. Walter was on leave for most of that week and on the Saturday afternoon we went to the cinema. We walked home in spite of the rain, to help pass the time; I remember it because I fretted about it when I found the telegram from the hospital waiting for me. It said that my sister was seriously ill.

I could not understand why I was being notified unless, as Walter said, I was meant to go to Bristol. But I did not think that I could visit Anne without her permission. I did not want to listen to Walter: she was my sister and the telegram was addressed to me and by now I thought too little of him to find it acceptable that he should know better about anything, understand more than myself. Nowadays one would think at once of telephoning the hospital. Perhaps we thought making a trunk call from a public call box too difficult, or perhaps what we thought too difficult was getting further information over the telephone. Or perhaps telephoning did not even occur to us.

The post office was shut and I could not get at my savings. I had what was left of my week's wages (thirty-five shillings before deductions) after paying my rent (one pound including electricity and coal). Most of what money Walter had saved for his leave we had by now spent. I did not want him to come with me to Bristol—if I was going—but he would not hear of letting his "little woman" make that journey alone. My parents were by whom I wanted to be looked after, my sisters were with whom I wanted to share; I did not understand it at the time, but I was keeping them unreplaced in my life as if I were practising witchcraft to get them back.

It would not have worried me, even under the circumstances, if I had arrived in Bristol penniless: I constantly felt so insecure that having money made only a little difference, and only in ways which did not really matter to me. I know from experience that I could always manage, not because I was capable but because I had to. Walter pointed out that we would need money also for somewhere to stay.

He took my telegram and went off, to the police station, to an army welfare office. I packed a small suitcase and when he came back with, I think, twenty pounds we went to the station. The next train south was not going to leave for so long that it would have been more sensible to go back home—we had not eaten since lunch-time. Walter suggested it; I was not doing anything for Anne by making things harder for myself, he said, not understanding that what made the situation bearable for me was its drama. I needed to remain at the station and be hungry. He bought himself a sandwich; he ate it ostentatiously in front of me but failed in his purpose to make me want to have one, too.

Earlier, he had annoyed me by insisting that Anne's condition justified my rushing to her; now he annoyed me by trying to make the occasion seem ordinary. Of course I was upset and of course it helped me to be upset merely with him. Throughout the journey he tried to reassure me; perhaps it could not be done, but I hated him for not being able to do it.

Had we gone home, we would have found a second telegram, stating that Anne was dangerously ill, and providing an authorisation for travel warrants for myself and another person to accompany me.

We arrived in Bristol towards noon. Walter enquired the way; his accent sounded (to me) worse than mine, but it was less likely to arouse hostility because he was in uniform. He was told that, as it was on Sunday, few buses were running and it was too far to walk. We decided to take a taxi; it was the first time either of us had ever done so.

"Won't be long now," he said. Throughout the night and all morning, he had been commenting on the passage of time, presumably for the sake of saying something. How could he not have noticed, known, that I did not like it? It sounded patronising to me.

He said, "We haven't got anything for her, fruit or flowers; we ought to have tried to buy something at the station." What was the good of thinking of it now? Since it was too late he ought to have left it unsaid; it served only to increase my anxiety about Anne's response to seeing me: it was this and not her condition which I was worried about. I half expected her to tell me to go away and not come back until she asked me to. Not for a moment did I believe that it had been her idea to send for me: I was totally unconvinced that I mattered that much to her.

We found our way to the right building and within it, to the right ward. Outside its double swing doors we were told that it was not visiting time. At that point even Walter had the tact not to say that we had been sent for. We had come all the way from Edinburgh, he said. We were allowed to go in.

I remember the ward as being huge, as being big enough to hold at least twenty and perhaps as many as thirty beds. Anne was occupying the third or it may have been the fourth one on the right hand side. I don't remember if we were shown to it or if I needed to find it for myself. Perhaps it was merely pointed out to us—wartime shortages must have affected also the number of nurses—"See the stand with the bag of blood."

I thought that getting the transfusion was what was keeping her lying so still. Her head was on only one pillow; all the rest of her was covered up. Her face, including her lips, was colourless; her eyes were open but unseeing until they focused on me. Perhaps it was drugs that made their blue seem faded. She must after all have known that I was coming; she appeared to be unsurprised that I was there.

In spite of the telegram, it did not occur to me that she

might die; even seeing her thus I did not fear for her life. I believed that I had been sent for because it was normal for people in hospitals to have visitors, and what friends she had were all in the services, which left only me, as a civilian, available, and also, that the authorities, with the lack of understanding I was used to from the British, would have assumed that her little sister was the one person whom Anne would most want to see. It did not occur to me that she might die because this was an unthinkable thought.

"You're wearing lipstick," she said. I told her that I was not. "Oh yes, you are," she insisted. Perhaps it was an illusion created by the effect on my face of the almost sleepless night, the emotional havoc. In the context of our relationship, it was a reassuring way for her to greet me.

She greeted Walter more conventionally. I would rather he had not been there; from when I had found the telegram I had wished to disencumber myself of him and not known how to do it. Anne, even then, managed it within a few minutes. First she told him to get me a chair; then she told him to go and buy me something to read, not a newspaper because of the noise it would make when I turned the pages, but a book, two or three books, because he might be mistaken in thinking that he knew what I would like: so as to relieve her of the obligation to entertain me while I sat there beside her. She also apologized to him for spoiling his leave.

Quite early in the evening, as the ward was being got ready for the night, one of the nurses going off duty came to Anne's bed and told Walter and me that, if we were to come with her, she would help us to find somewhere to stay.

Through the blackout, she took us to a nearby boarding house, telling us that we would be able to get supper there; we had not sat down to a meal since Saturday lunch-time. The manageress asked us, as she was obliged to do by law, to show our papers before signing the register. When she saw my Aliens Registration Book she told not us but the nurse that we could not stay: her rooms were full of the relatives of people who were war casualties, especially airmen: she owed it to them not to take in a German national. She was willing to stretch a point for Walter, because at least he was in uniform and he was after all an Austrian. Perhaps she did not believe that we were married, I looked too young. I would have accepted being turned away rather than let the woman see me cry, with vexation and exhaustion more than self-pity. But the nurse continued to argue on my behalf and, eventually, the manageress agreed to let me stay for that one night on condition that I did not use the dining-room.

I was past being hungry for English food.

The next morning, while I went off to the hospital, Walter went in search of somewhere else for me to stay; it was the last day of his leave. He found a room in a nearby housing-estate. He had paid the rent for a week, he told me, as he took me to see where it was, and the landlady was not interested in my nationality. It was quite a nice room but it did not really matter what it was like; I would need it only for sleeping.

"Let's try out the bed," Walter said, with the look, between roguishness and shame, which always made explicit whatever euphemism he was using for having sex. He could not possibly get back to his unit by midnight, therefore it did not matter if he did not catch the next train. . . .

It mattered to me to get back to the hospital. I thought that it would be indecent to indulge our bodies here in Bristol, to which we had come because Anne was lying ill. I understood that what Walter was after was less his own sexual gratification than the satisfaction of knowing that he had comforted me, and I did not want to be comforted, neither by him nor by means of having sex; I did not want to have sex with him. He did not seem to realise it, or else he believed that I was refusing him for no valid reason, or that he knew better than I did what was good for me. When he continued to insist I gave in to him; I lay down on the bed and let him do as he wished, because I needed to see my partner as dominant. It suited my emotional make-up but not my body; I found the occasion physically unpleasant and from then on having sex with Walter was repugnant to me.

After Anne's death, in answer to my enquiry, the hospital authorities wrote me a letter explaining that she had suffered from purpura, an extremely rare condition which meant that her blood had lost its capacity to clot. The operation in which her spleen had been removed was experimental: if it failed to cure her she was bound to bleed to death. The alternative, she had been told, would have been to live on as an invalid, with no hope of recovery. She chose.

She lacked the energy and the will to explain this to me and she had always discouraged me from asking her questions: if she knew something which she wanted me to know she would tell it to me unasked. What inhibited me from asking the ward sister was the fear of arousing Anne's displeasure by talking about her to a stranger. But I needed to write to my employer to explain my continuing absence from work, I needed to give him some idea of how much longer I would be away; there were wartime regulations about absenteeism. I mentioned this to Anne and she told me that the doctor made his round on Tuesday mornings; she wanted me in any case to talk with him.

He said, "I suggest that you stay for the rest of the week, I think that by then we shall all be feeling happy about your sister." Not a word of warning.

He was a very handsome, still youngish man, and because Anne had been impatient for his coming I wondered if perhaps she was a little in love with him. So unrealistic were my thoughts about her.

Writing to me of her "small operation," she had joked about the preciousness of her blood; it was of a rare type. Not knowing then that having had jaundice as a child disqualified mine, I offered to have it tested for compatibility with Anne's and was chagrined to be told that she did not need another transfusion. Just the same, she continued to lie still, her face wan, her eyes when she opened them without animation. Occasionally, she offered me her hand; it was without strength. Occasionally, she said, "Talk to me." And I found things to talk about until she drifted back into unconsciousness or sleep. Occasionally, she asked me, "Aren't you bored?" And I answered that I wasn't. She wouldn't have liked it if I had reminded her that throughout my twenty years, being with her was what I had always liked best; whenever I had said or shown how much I loved her she had called it moral blackmail.

I sat by her bed and for much of the time I read. *Lost Horizon, Good-bye, Mr. Chips,* which were best-sellers just then, and like Walter I believed that I ought to like them. That they weren't to my taste made me think less not of them but of myself.

Several times in the course of each day, Anne or one of the nurses sent me away while the screens were placed round her bed for what needed to be done. I made use of those intervals to go to the lavatory and to the canteen. Or I hung about the corridor until I was invited into the kitchen; I was told that I could come in there at any time and help myself to a cup of tea. All the staff: the sisters, the nurses, the auxiliaries were friendly; they were friendlier than I expected them to be, friendlier than I was used to strangers being, in England; I believed that this was because Anne was liked so much by everybody that they were being nice to me for her sake.

On the Tuesday evening, she did not want me to leave because, she told me, the previous night she had been in too much pain to sleep, and the night nurse had been unable to reach the doctor for authorisation to increase her dose of morphine. If she should once more spend a sleepless night she wanted me to keep her company.

Never before in the whole of my life—with the exception of the recent night in which she had shared my bed—had she shown any sign of needing me. It did not alarm me, that she was no longer too proud; it made me happy.

It did not alarm me that the nurses let me make up a bed for myself in an empty side ward. There I slept, not much further away from Anne than when we had still been at home. She also slept through until morning.

The following night we spent the same way and then it was Thursday.

As so often, I was not fully aware of what was going on around me. But I overheard a nurse saying that "an old woman at the far end" had died in the night. Until then I had been able to believe that dying people were elsewhere in the hospital, that this surgical ward was only for those who were recovering. And Anne was showing some small signs of it: she spent more time awake, talked more, told me that she was hoping to be chosen as a helper by one of the Zionist leaders in rescue missions.

I was further reassured when, that morning, the bed on her right was given to an eight-year-old girl who had had her tonsils out. Sitting facing Anne, I had my back to her; but I turned round and talked to the child, offered to do things for her. As always, my wish to be of use was hampered by my fear of being found inadequate; but I tried to be helpful to the nurses, believing that my continuing presence depended on their goodwill.

I kept thinking how lucky I was to be allowed to remain with Anne; I was amazed at everyone's kindness to me.

Anne had a cup with a spout from which to drink water; I held it for her and don't remember her drinking anything else or eating at all. That day, at lunch-time, when I wanted to go to the canteen, she told me to stay: I should go later, while the nurses were dealing with her. A week had passed since her operation and she was to be given a blanket-bath and to have her bed-linen and her nightdress changed. But when it came to it she told me, "Don't go far," and, as I had done all my life, I obeyed her.

I remained just outside the ward, increasingly aware that I needed to relieve my bladder. I would have had ample time to go to the block of public lavatories; but I did not know this until after I had been in the corridor for so long that I thought, any moment now Anne will be expecting me back. She had conditioned me not to keep her waiting.

It was twenty minutes past two by the clock on the wall when I ambled into the kitchen. Standing beneath it, the sister was speaking into the telephone; I heard her say, "Have I ever called you to an emergency that wasn't one?" I thought, now surely the nurses will have to finish with Anne. I went to take another look through the windows in the swing doors and saw that the screens were still about her bed. As the sister brushed past me I asked her, "How much longer—" before I saw that the doctor was already with her. He was so romantically handsome that I could not help telling myself stories about him.

If she answered me I don't remember what she said. They did not go anywhere else: they went behind the screens about Anne's bed. Not until I saw them doing this did I begin to fear for her; and still I thought—so stubbornly hopeful, so young was I—that to cope with emergencies was what doctors and nurses were for, that they were doing so all the time and afterwards people recovered.

A nurse came from behind the screens; she was looking for me and found me on the far side of the swing doors. The expression on her face was bland. "You can go back now," she said, and still I wondered why, while the screens were remaining in place.

As I had been doing over and over again during the past ninety-seven and a half hours, I walked round the foot of the bed to Anne's right side. She looked just as she had before, except that there was spittle between her lips, stirred into froth as she breathed, and she was breathing at intervals, at ever increasing intervals. And then she stopped breathing.

Standing opposite me, the doctor who had been bending over her straightened up. The nurse who had been busy with the blood-transfusion apparatus desisted. The doctor folded his stethoscope and said to me, "I am sorry."

He left. The nurses left, closing the gaps between the screens through which they had gone, the one with the blood-transfusion apparatus taking it with her. I was left alone with Anne.

I was being given time. For what? To get used to the thought of her death? I have not got used to it after almost half a century. I still weep for her; I write this weeping. But then I wept almost not at all. A nurse, looking in on me, came closer to pat my shoulder and to say, "She wouldn't want you to cry."

I was in no state to decide whether or not this was true. With Anne no longer able to order me about, I accepted what a stranger told me on her behalf. I stopped crying, instantly, unable to comprehend that she was no longer there.

I thought of kissing Anne, her cheek, even her lips; I thought about touching her near shoulder where the flesh was bare—her hands were under the blankets, her arms covered up. (Her fresh nightdress, light blue, was sleeveless with narrow straps.) I wanted to touch her because I wished her to know that as far as I was concerned nothing between us had changed: but just because nothing had changed for me I could not do it; never in my life had I touched her without her consent. To do so now would have meant unfairly taking advantage of her state.

I had not before encountered death sufficiently closely to have given it enough thought. I did not know what to think of it, was doubtful about what it meant. I had grown up believing in the existence of the human soul; that I no longer believed in a personal God did not mean that I felt bound to believe that nothing of Anne except her body survived. I felt free to believe as I chose about myself, but about her I felt that I was committed to believing as she had done. And though there was nothing we had not at one time or another talked about, I did not know with what belief she had been facing her death.

I could not negate her soul in case it existed: if it existed she would know my thoughts; I had always endeavoured to please her and more than ever wanted to do so now. It was as if I believed that if Anne expected to have an immortal soul then she would have one. Not even her death had shaken my faith in her.

I wanted there to be something, anything, I could still do for her. Now more than ever I needed her, or Lise, or our parents, to tell me or to show me what to do. To close her eyes seemed to me to be such a violation of the autonomy of what remained of her that I refrained from doing it for what seemed a very long time. I did so, eventually, only because I thought that she might have expected it of me, and would have wanted it to be done even less by a stranger.

Her jaw had sagged open. When a nurse—the same or another one—looked in on me, I asked her if something could not be done about this. She fetched an ice-bag with which to prop up Anne's chin. This seemed to me to be a worse indignity and I made her take it away.

The previous day or the day before it, an army chaplain had come to the bedside; he had needed to tell me that he was a rabbi or I would not have known it—he was clean-shaven and young. We had exchanged a few words. He came now; I wondered at his fortuitous presence in the hospital. He stood at the foot of the bed briefly in silence, and then suggested that I should leave with him. It did not occur to me that he had come also for my benefit. I told him that I wanted to stay and he left.

It did not occur to me at the time that the screens served the purpose of sparing the other patients the sight of Anne's death and my devastation. I thought how extraordinarily considerate of me people were being to allow me to go on sitting there with her in privacy. But presumably the hospital porter came as soon as he could. Anne was placed on his trolley and her face, her whole head, all of her was covered up with a sheet. I asked him if I might come with them and was grateful when he said yes.

He took her not to a passenger but a service lift. It seemed to me to be a terrible aspect of her death, this different way in which, as soon as it had happened, she had begun to be treated.

From the exit we walked, slightly downhill, past other buildings, in the open air. It was an ordinary August afternoon and the world looked the same as always. It made me draw emotionally even closer to her than I had ever dared to do while she lived; I think I was trying to fuse her identity with mine so as to keep her alive. I thought of helping to push the trolley but did not because it was taking her to be relegated.

There were several biers, covered with black velvet, on the floor of the mortuary chapel, leaving a space for her against one of the walls, under an altar with lit candles below either—I don't remember which—a cross or a crucifix. Our grandfather (our mother's father, who had been the only grandfather we knew) had been by German-Jewish standards an orthodox man. Our mother had been an only child and Anne had been his first and favourite granddaughter. There must have been in my mind an echo of his influence on my childhood beliefs, something about people being reunited in death, perhaps the memory of the story of the death of King David's baby. Because it was our grandfather I thought of. I was used to living in an ostensibly Christian environment, was so used to its symbols that I could ignore them. But I did not want the responsibility of ignoring this one on Anne's and our grandfather's behalf.

"I don't want her to lie there," I said, and could not explain why, assuming the porter to be a Christian and not wanting to offend him. But when he saw by my face that it mattered to me, he made space for Anne's bier away from the altar. "She won't be in here for long," he said, and I closed my mind against thoughts of what this meant.

What seemed also terrible to me was that, all the while Anne was dying and I was grieving, my body clamoured for attention to its needs. The porter and I, retracing our steps, he pushing his empty trolley, again passed the block of public lavatories; this time I went into it and my emotions felt shamed.

I returned to the ward, partly because I could not think what else to do, where else to go, but chiefly because I wanted to be with people who had known Anne; the only thing about myself which mattered to me just then was that I had lost her and they knew that too. I think they must have been looking out for me; next to the ward kitchen was a linen-room, with three women working in it, one perhaps the matron; they took charge of me. And tried to comfort me with a cup of tea, too strong and much too sweet even for my taste; I did not want it but I wanted even less to reject their kindness.

Perhaps they had been told to hold on to me. Someone, a doctor perhaps, came with a piece of paper authorising an autopsy; it needed my signature. He explained that the condition which Anne had suffered from was so rare that little was known about it; they needed this chance to learn, it might one day help someone else. He went on trying to persuade me, who was already persuaded; I knew before he told me so that this was what Anne would have wanted. It did not occur to me that he anticipated a problem because we—Anne and I—were Jews. The way I saw it, I did not cause people problems because I was Jewish: it was because I was that other people caused problems for me.

And then I was asked to remove Anne's belongings from the bedside locker; the bed had already been stripped and remade. I did not want to do it; it seemed to me, whom she had never allowed to touch her things, to be an exploitation of her powerlessness. There were no plastic bags then; they must have given me some sort of container, into which I emptied the shelves as much as possible without looking at anything. So against the grain did this go with me that I don't remember carrying these spoils when I left the hospital. Yet no doubt I cherished as having belonged to Anne even the least of them.

While I was waiting at the bus stop the rabbi joined me; I thought by coincidence but now I am not so sure. Where was I going? he asked and I told him, to the post office, to write to my other sister.

I had stopped writing to her years before, because the exchange of letters took so long that hers were always out of step with my life, and anyway everything always needed too much explaining. Letters served only to exacerbate our separation and the truth is that I hated her for leaving me, who still needed her so much and missed her so, and for having been able to make another life for herself in which I had no part. But when Anne had told me, in Edinburgh, that she was exchanging letters with Lise, whom I had always seen less as her sister than mine, I was jealous. I got her address—I had not even known where she was—and had been meaning to write to her ever since.

It would soon be closing time at the post office, the rabbi pointed out; I should leave going there until the morning and we could have a meal together, his treat. He wanted to pay my fare on the bus—a penny was all it cost—but I would not let him: I was still poor or perhaps merely insecure enough for a penny to matter to me, and as neither my parents nor my sisters could do anything for me, I preferred to have nothing done for me rather than have it done by strangers.

In those days, letters abroad to places like Palestine needed to be written on special forms, conveyed as microfilm and printed at the other end much reduced in size. Therefore, one needed to make one's writing large and could not fit much onto a page. I wrote in English, well aware that Lise hardly understood it; it was still a foreign language to me, too. I think I was using it to distance myself from what I was saying; in the language of our childhood I could not have told her *in a letter*—in forced handwriting—that Anne was dead. Yet I needed her to know it as much as if her knowing it could have made a difference. To the three of us.

I had the room which Walter had rented for me; it did not prevent me from feeling homeless in Bristol. I had met a few people there but I knew no one. I spent most of the next three days wandering by myself about the streets to pass the time between what I needed to do.

On Friday morning, I met the rabbi as agreed on the steps of the registry office to have Anne's death recorded. I wanted to do it myself, by myself, as one of the few things I could still do for her, though had the rabbi not told me I would not have known that this was something which needed to be done. And I did not even know the cause of her death. When the rabbi told it to him, the registrar did not accept it: in his long years in office he had never heard of it; he looked it up in a reference book and also telephoned the hospital, before writing it down. Anne was one in a million even in what she died of.

On Friday afternoon, I went back to the hospital. The rabbi had told me that two of the women who performed this service for the Bristol Jewish community would be preparing her body for burial and that, if I wished, I would be able to look at her lying in her coffin. I did not want to do this, did not want to have to remember this as my last sight of her. Again, it seemed to me to be an abominable intrusion into her privacy; I did not think that she would have approved of it. But I could not be sure of this and it was expected of me and so I waited in the porter's lodge until I was summoned.

Into a white-tiled place with, all along one wall, something like a row of filing cabinets, of I think metal, but larger and also white. Coffin-sized drawers with, above or below or between the handles, small fixtures for holding the constantly changed labels naming the bodies stored within. I was glad that the coming of the Sabbath had necessitated Anne being taken out of there quickly.

And there she was lying, in a lidless coffin on the floor at my feet, covered up almost to her shoulders with a sheet so that no more of her was to be seen than when she had been lying in her hospital bed. Her head, the whole shape of her looked smaller than I had remembered and her skin was no longer white like our mother's as it had been in life. Her skin was yellow and she looked no bigger than I.

On Saturday morning I went to the synagogue. I could not have made myself betray to strangers in the street that I was a Jew by asking where it was; I must have asked the two old women—old to me who was so young—who had laid out Anne. At home, the Friday night service was the one I had loved best;

but perhaps what I could not face was only the walking through unfamiliar streets in the blackout.

I opened a ground-floor door and was denied entry by a man who waved me away, up the stairs to the women's gallery. I did not then know that this traditional separation of the sexes during prayers was intended to avoid people being distracted by carnal thoughts; I believed that it was due to men thinking women less worthy. (At home, we had had a women's gallery, too; it was used only on the High Holy Days, when the whole community attended and there was not enough seating downstairs.)

"No women in here" was too much like *Juden verboten* (forbidden to Jews). I almost left.

I felt as alienated as if it had been a church, in this synagogue in which all that was different from what I had been used to mattered more to me than whatever was the same. I burned with homesickness and with being alone. This was the occasion when, for the first time, I felt the guilt which is said to be a common feeling with survivors; I did not know that another in my place would also have felt it: I believed that feeling so guilty meant that I was.

After the sermon, the rabbi (the rabbi of the Bristol community) announced the funeral of "a girl soldier without family"; all available men should attend to make sure of a minyan (ten adult males required for communal prayers). At the Fishponds cemetery, on Sunday afternoon, at three o'clock.

Until then I had not known when or where Anne's funeral would be.

I sought the rabbi out, after the service, to tell him that there was a sister; I think what was important to me was that he should know that Anne had not been as alone as I was.

I also needed to ask him where the cemetery was. He told me that I should come to his house, next to the synagogue, and we would go there together.

But I was anxious to see where Anne would lie. As, before her arrival in Edinburgh, I had gone to inspect the attic, after leaving the synagogue—ignoring that it was lunch-time—I found the bus which would take me out to the Fishponds.

I was used to cemeteries which were landscaped like parks; there Jews had still been able to take a walk unmolested even in Nazi Germany, and we had done so, often. The cemetery in which Anne was to be buried looked to me like a wasteland: a walled plot no larger than a couple of allotments, gently sloping away from the locked gates. Among the wild-growing grass were small, plain headstones, set closely together, rows upon rows of them.

I spent the rest of Saturday afternoon wandering about the city centre, much of the time thinking of mourning clothes.

When my mother's mother had died, my mother had put on mourning; she was still wearing it when her father died: he had been the president of the local Jewish community and was its first victim of the Nazis. Afterwards she continued to wear black: in mourning, she used to say, for the Jews of Germany.

The only coat I owned was the fawn raincoat which Walter had bought for me, three years before, the first time we had been together since we had left Germany. And I had a headscarf, as was the wartime fashion, which had a paisley pattern the dominant colour of which was blood-red. There was no time to get my coat dyed. Again, it was Saturday afternoon: the post office was closed and I did not have the cash to buy another; I did not have the necessary clothing coupons. I thought about it, obsessively, as if it mattered, perhaps so as not to have to think about Anne's death.

I thought about buying at least a black scarf or beret. I could not make myself go into a shop and do it. Psychologists say that we often mistake our motives. I had grown up hearing that Jews were, among other things, stingy; I believed that I grudged spending money and coupons on something I would wear only once. But now I think the truth was that I did not want to put on mourning for Anne as the only way I had of punishing her for having deserted me.

On Sunday morning, my landlady brought my breakfast on a

tray to my room, and invited me to have lunch with her and her children; her husband was serving in North Africa. I had told her that Anne was dead. I did not want her to know—perhaps because I had no mourning clothes—that the funeral was to be that afternoon. When I went into the kitchen in mid-morning to offer my help, I told her that I had an appointment at half past two and she told me, what I ought to have remembered from the previous Sunday, that there were few buses on that day between Southmead and the city centre. I should allow well over an hour, she said.

I would have preferred to set out at once but she would not hear of it: she would get the food ready as quickly as possible, serve it up early; perhaps she felt her world threatened by the glimpse she caught of the one I was living in. I could not cope with her distress in addition to mine. I stayed to eat the meal, including the Yorkshire pudding which had after all delayed it, because she had forgotten how long it took, having not troubled to make it since her husband had been away. I forced it down, disliking the taste of it. But, thinking ahead, I refused the inevitable cup of tea. And ran all the way to the bus stop.

The rabbi and I met in the street: he was coming away from his house. For the rest of the afternoon, now and again, compulsively, I kept thinking, what would I have done if I had missed him? As appalled by what had almost happened as if I believed that it could still matter to Anne whether or not I attended her funeral.

We congregated at a nearby bus stop: half a dozen or so men in dark coats and Homburg hats and this small, pale, sad-eyed, tongue-tied girl in bright clothing, a maverick among Jews as well as non-Jews, in England.

When it was almost three o'clock, the men decided to take a taxi, sharing the cost. The sky was overcast, the wind cold for August. While we were on our way it started to rain.

Waiting for us in the cemetery were four people in uniform: the army chaplain, Anne's commanding officer, and two girls who claimed to have been her friends. There was also the nurse who had caught up with me on Friday afternoon, as I was leaving the hospital grounds after my last look at Anne. She told me that, before the operation, Anne had been in her ward and they had made friends. Nurses were not supposed to do that, she had explained, nor to attend a patient's funeral; but she had liked Anne so much that she would come to it if I would let her know when it was. I had not done so. I had of course written to Walter that Anne had died, but delayed posting the letter so that he would not get it in time to come, supposing he could have got compassionate leave. I did not want him there; I wanted none of them there; I would have preferred the occasion to have been one between just Anne and me.

I had never before attended a funeral; the presence of so many strangers changed it for me from what it ought to have meant into a social ordeal.

Anne was waiting for us in her coffin, in the small building just inside the gates; we trooped into it for prayers. Somebody whispered, "No flowers." Until then it had not registered with me; I did not know whether there were no flowers because it was wartime, or because it was not the custom with Jews in England to have them, or because to provide them had been my responsibility and I had failed in it. The coffin was covered starkly with—perhaps it ought to have been a prayer shawl and perhaps it was one, but I remember it as a tarpaulin. Beneath it, coiled on the lid, was the rope for lowering the coffin into the ground; I did not realise what it was. From wondering about this protuberance I went on to wonder if Anne was in that coffin, if I had really seen her die, or if what I thought was happening, the whole world, existed only in so far as I believed that it did.

Some of the men hoisted the coffin onto their shoulders to carry it, in the summer rain, the few yards to its grave. Before they stepped over the threshold, one of them turned his head and asked, "Who is the sister?" Throughout our childhood I had wanted to be not the third but the first; now I was that and I did not want to be. I thought that if Anne had been there—

she was: if she had been able to see how I was behaving, she would have been very critical of me; she always had been and I had never given her more cause.

And then it occurred to me that if her soul had survived she would be able to do more than see me: she would know what was in my heart and mind as if she were God. I had ceased to believe in God but supposing that I was wrong? At that moment, I did not fear him and his Judgment Day as much as I feared Anne's soul being able to know me in all my inadequacy. That she had died, having had for her life no more than these particular twenty-two years, seemed infinitely sad; I thought it even sadder that she had only me to be her chief mourner. It may have been my way of missing our mother, our father, and Lise; that did not occur to me perhaps because, emotionally, I could not afford to think of them just then. I was conscious of myself not being enough and believed that this was due to my being who I was.

Of traditional Hebrew prayers, in their unfamiliar English pronunciation, I understood very little. Her commanding officer said a few sentences in English to which I closed my ears. As I afterwards closed them to whatever was said about her by the two ATS girls who had been her friends. I had always had the feeling that I was not part of Anne's life as she was of mine. I did not want to hear about this life of hers which I had not been a part of. I was not interested in other people's reminiscence of her, the world's Anne. For all my feelings of inferiority I believed that I loved her enough to be the best keeper of her memory.

A TEMPERED WIND

December 15, 1938–January 1939

(Dovercourt)

The ferry docked in the course of the night but we were not allowed on deck until it was daylight. Our first sight of England was Harwich. More important to me at that moment was the woman who was standing at the top of the gangway, directing us children to the right and to the left, alternately. I had believed that I had left fear behind but now I feared that my sister and I would be separated and, among all those strangers, would be unable to find each other again. I made Lise let go of my hand to take hers instead: I knew from experience that I was better than she at getting my own way. She was not much more than a year older than I, who had turned fifteen at the end of August. I liked to think that I was her equal; I would have resented it had I known that our mother had made her promise to look after me. Nevertheless, she was my security.

We did not look like sisters: she was very thin, with a narrow, pale face, straight silky black hair and our father's brown eyes; my eyes are grey, my face is round, my hair coarse and then it was dark brown and wavy. Naturally, she was taller than I, but I looked stronger.

We were allowed to walk on together.

And were confronted with two women, one with a list on which she ticked off the names, the other with cardboard labels on string to hang about our necks. I needed to nudge Lise, she was so shy, so that she would give her name before I gave mine. *K* coming before *L,* my number came before hers and this felt so wrong to me that as soon as we had walked on I made her exchange labels.

We had to be passed by a doctor. "Open your mouth," I was told. I pretended not to understand what was wanted of me even when it was made plain with gestures: every doctor who had ever looked down my throat had found fault with my tonsils. I believed that because of them—if they did not matter then why was the doctor looking?—I might not be allowed to land.

That fear, too, had been needless.

Ours was the second of the children's transports from Nazi Germany, which were the response of the British people (and the French, Dutch, and Danish) to the November pogrom. Our arrival was news; reporters were waiting on the quayside. I had been learning English for more than a year and joined the children who were trying to talk with them. "My father is in a concentration camp," a boy was saying, and others, girls too, joined in as if agreeing with him: their fathers or uncles or older brothers were in concentration camps too. Somebody said, "My father was beaten up and killed." There was a hush, and into it another boy said, "The Nazis won't stop until all the Jews left in Germany have been killed." Perhaps he did not use exactly those words, but they mean what I understood him to say, and though I did not know who he was, I believed him.

It had never occurred to me that my parents' lives were in danger. I had not found it difficult to leave them: I had left them before, to go to children's holiday homes and to go to boarding school. I had thought that this time I would be merely further away. Until that moment I had not realised that this parting was different and might be forever.

I still dream of being in the reception camp at Dovercourt. I am cold to the tips of my fingers and my toes; outside it is snowing and in the main building it is the body-heat of so many children which keeps the temperature above freezing, rather than the stoves; their heat goes into the wet clothing hung all over the fireguards. Children are milling about and somewhere among them is Lise. I am looking for her, she may well be close without my knowing it: too many other children are between us. It's no good calling her name, there is so much noise that she won't be able to hear it. I push through to the smaller hall, where there is always less pandemonium. The piano is being played in there by some musically gifted child but it isn't Lise.

If she found me gone from where we had last been together, she may have thought that I have decided to go to bed. I can't find my coat; if I went out into the night without it perhaps the cold would kill me, and I am tempted. Eventually, I find it: under so many other coats that it is still wet.

Outside, the beauty of the scene—the falling snow, the glistening lights—is as hurtful to my spirit as the cold air is to my lungs: it's hard to want not to be alive when the world is so beautiful. The rows of huts all look the same, with washrooms and lavatories at the corners; the huts all look more or less the same, though some sleep four in bunks, some two in single beds. I have forgotten the number and cannot find the hut to which Lise has moved us, in an attempt to staunch my homesickness by giving us the chance to be alone together. When at last I manage to find it she is not there.

She has decorated the walls with pictures cut from magazines and the window-sill with holly in a jam jar. I hate her for not feeling as I do, rebellious; for always being willing to make the best of things. I don't want to be comforted by her. I fear that if I let go of the need I feel for my mother it will make me lose her.

The air is as cold within as it is without. This is a holiday camp meant for summer occupation. I don't want to get into the bed with its English blankets instead of a duvet. I don't want to go to sleep and wake up in exile.

I leave the light burning as a signal to Lise, and close the door thoroughly to contain all that we can at the moment call ours. I can hear the sea roaring. The site slopes down to it. It starts no more than two dozen or so steps beyond the camp lights. I think that because this place is called Dovercourt we must be close to Dover, and fantasize crossing the Channel back to my parents. The sea is wild and I cannot swim; I think, if God wills it. But I lack the faith in him to put it to the test.

It is not a dream at all but a composite memory which comes back to me sometimes while I sleep.

Within the first few days—before it started to snow: the sun was shining—Lise and I, going from our hut to the main building, were stopped by one of the staff with a sheaf of papers. "Have you filled in one of these?" she asked, and repeated herself in halting German, showing us that what she was holding were questionnaires. She explained that she was a student at London University; this was her Christmas vacation and she had come as a volunteer in the hope of improving her German. But she had been told to encourage us children to speak English. "I wouldn't have bothered to come if I'd known," she said, laughing; perhaps it was meant to be a joke.

She could not have been much older than we, but to us she was a young woman, in her casual tweeds, with her grown-up hairstyle and high heels, and with above all that self-assurance which distinguished the adults from the children and the Britishers among the staff from those who were also refugees.

She was cheerful, practising her German on us because our English proved to be inadequate, and pleased to discover that we were sisters because this simplified her task. So our father was an architect? Looking at our shabby coats, she waited for us to confirm it before writing it down, twice. "But he hasn't been that for the past five years," we told her. Pencil poised, she looked up with genuine interest, asking, "So what has he been doing?" Lise and I looked at each other, unwilling to shame him by citing the means to which he had had to resort to provide even marginally for his family. "Well, never mind," she said, kindly. "It isn't really—" and did not know the German word for "relevant."

"Now, what about your schooling?" she asked Lise; I had insisted, to both of them, that as the elder she must be asked first. She made a poor impression when she was embarrassed. "Until you left home, you were still at school?" the young woman prompted. Arm in arm with Lise, I could feel her beginning to tremble. Afterwards she told me that she had been daunted by the thought of all that had needed explaining. For the past one and a half years she had been an apprentice dressmaker.

When she had at last got this out, the young woman, writing it down, commented, "Very nice." But the tone of her voice betrayed what she thought of it. It was what we thought of it, too; but even I knew that there was no point in saying so. "So this is what you want to be, a dressmaker?" she asked Lise.

"Oh no," my cowed and optimistic sister said. "What I would really like to be is a doctor."

And I, who liked to pretend that we were twins, had not known it.

"It has always seemed so impossible," she explained to me afterwards why she had never told me. But now that we were in England . . .

It was impossible still. "I can't put that down," the young woman filling in the form said. "You must remember that you are a refugee."

I had believed that we had come to England in order to escape being discriminated against. If we were still not to be like other children, then what had we got to compensate us for having left our parents?

Lise, as always trying to please no matter whom, asked if it was acceptable for her to say that she wanted to be a teacher. She was good with children, having all my life practised on me.

Enraged by her meekness, I pointed out that it didn't matter what she said as we were on our way to the Land of Israel.

I received an icy smile to cool my feelings. "I was told to fill in these forms and so I must do it," the young woman said. She put Lise's form underneath to complete mine.

I had been attending the German branch of a progressive Jewish boarding school which had been evacuated to England by its founder in 1933. I had had a scholarship to it. Since coming to Dovercourt, I had decided not even to try for a place in the English school because I could not bear the thought of being parted from Lise. I had not discussed this with her for fear that she would try to make me change my mind. I hated it when she disagreed with me; worse: I then hated not the disagreement but Lise. It did not happen often.

What I was going to be I already was: a writer. My mother used to say, "How can you make poems in the language in which we are being cursed!" It wasn't a question because it had no answer. At that time I believed that, eventually, I would be writing in Hebrew—a language in which, through synagogue services and atavistically, I was at least emotionally at home. What self-esteem had been left to me by the Nazi environment consisted of my ability to write; I had already had poems published in the children's supplement of the national Jewish newspaper, the only outlet available to me.

I was not going to expose my talent, the most important thing about me, to the comment of this young woman. Asked what I wanted to be I said, on the spur of the moment, "A gardener." German romantic poetry had taught me to appreciate nature. But it was meant as a joke, and to see it written down on my form was a sort of victory. What was not known about me was inviolable.

Lise and I attended the Friday night service, less because we believed in God—though we did—than because we knew that in its ritual we would feel at home. Before it, we changed into white blouses and navy blue skirts: the Zionist uniform. We put on our Stars of David, the only jewelry we owned. Our mother had had mine made out of the lid of her father's pocket watch; it was paper-thin and scored with what remained of his initials; the excess gold had paid for the cutting of it and for a flimsy gold chain. Lise's was a conventional one and I therefore thought it better; she wore it on a black cord. We had wanted to have them once the idea of Zionism had mitigated for us the hurt of being

Jews, and we had worn them openly in Germany. Lise could be recognised as a Jew by her ugly nose. I could have passed; but though I would very much rather not have been Jewish, I never tried to conceal it—until after I came to England.

By the time we returned to the hall, benches had been set out in rows in the far left hand corner. In front of them was a table covered with a white cloth, with two candlesticks; the candles had already been lit.

Lighting the Sabbath candles is one of the few observances which Jewish ritual allocates to girls and women; it was the sole action available there by which any girl could have domesticated the reception camp, tamed the confusion of it, turned its strangeness into home. Who had lit them? Would that it had been I! I was convinced that lighting them had not meant as much to the girl who had done it as it would have meant to me.

I asked Senta. She was the oldest girl in the camp, older than Lise. Since our arrival two days before, she had been seeking me out and I had welcomed her attention. A little willful self-deception allowed me to think that she was rather like Anne; she had some of her qualities, even some of her mannerisms. Indubitably, Senta knew how to be a big sister: she had a little sister who was still with their parents in Hamburg. And so we made do with each other.

It was Senta who had lit the candles. She wouldn't have done so but waited for me, she told me, had she known that I wanted to do it. Did I know the words of the Hebrew blessing which needed to be said? Senta was Orthodox and I had already told her that I wasn't.

"I know them," I told her, and she promised me that, the next Friday—if we were both still in Dovercourt—she would make sure that I would be the one to light the candles. And so I was.

The rabbi had come from London to take the service; he was also a German-speaking refugee. Sitting between Lise and Senta, participating in the familiar ritual, I felt momentarily safe. Behind us to our left, the trestle tables were being put up and set with a subdued clatter for the evening meal. The rest of the children were milling about; having been told to be quiet, they did not quite know what to do with themselves. There were also Gentiles, who were the children of active anti-Nazis, and children of Jewish descent who had been brought up as Christians. And Jewish children who did not believe in God.

Josefa Metz—she died in Theresienstadt—had been born in our home town; in the most famous of her children's poems a girl is saying her prayers, rather like Christopher Robin, asking for childish things. I knew it by heart and whenever I felt the urge to say a personal prayer, those words came into my mind, and I remembered that, according to Anne, this poem was not meant for children at all but was a sophisticated joke about children—and then I felt inhibited by shame. What arrogance, Anne had said, what presumption, to expect the creator of the universe—supposing that he existed—to concern himself with me! But saying the prescribed prayers, being said at sundown on Friday night by Jews all over the world, made me feel part of a whole which was great and important enough to matter even to God.

My mother used to say, "If God has chosen the Jews then he has chosen us for suffering."

In essence, every Jewish service is a thanksgiving; having completed the Hebrew prayers, the rabbi told us in German that we should give thanks. "Never forget," he said, "that other children might have come in your stead; by what you make of yourselves you must justify that, while they have remained behind to die, you have been saved."

I had not known that my life was being saved. I had believed that we had been brought out of Germany to spare us hardships. The rabbi's words echoed what the boy on the quayside had said, that all the Jews left in Germany would be killed. Did *they* know this, had they known it when they saw us off at the station? Why had they not warned us, why had my mother not told me, "Say good-bye to me properly, it may be for the last time"? I had broken out of her embrace and run from her, so impatient had I been to get on the train which was to take me to England.

Where it proved not to be true, what we had been told, that there we would be like everybody else: it might no longer matter that we were Jews, but now we were refugees. Moreover, we had become chosen children: chosen by God or by the people in the Reichsvertretung der Deutschen Juden (representative body of German Jewry) responsible for putting our names instead of those of other children on the emigration lists.

Senta, though she was a Zionist, was on her way to the United States; her father had relatives in Cleveland and was arranging for the whole family to go there. She felt unhappy about it but thought that she owed it to her parents to help them settle. All of us came to England on the understanding that we were only passing through: our visas were temporary, granted only to children with somewhere else to go to. We Zionists made use of this fact to argue that Jews were not wanted here either. As far as we were concerned, we had been allowed to come as an alternative to being allowed into Palestine.

So many youngsters now wanted to go there that Lise and I had, that autumn, been required to attend a month-long selection camp; we had been passed for places in a kibbutz or a children's village as soon as the Mandate authorities would grant us entry permits. Before we had been in Dovercourt for a week, there was an announcement over the loudspeakers that all children on their way to Palestine were to go into the small hall after lunch to meet with youth leaders from the London office of the Jewish Agency.

Of all the hundreds of children, not more than between fifty and sixty came to the meeting; it astonished me. So convinced was I in those days that the opinions held by the majority were the right ones and that therefore they would coincide with mine. I looked round at my fellow Zionists, with whom I had at least that much in common. It was at least possible that from at least some of them I would not be parted again. We were all looking at each other, open to making new friends.

There were three young men, who had kept their overcoats on and were talking among themselves, standing close to a wall, one with his back to us—as if we were of not much interest to them, who were so important to us. The one who eventually called for silence was fair-haired and blue-eyed and very handsome: Teddy Kollek, who was to become the mayor of Jerusalem.

These permits to enter the Land of Israel which we were waiting for, he began, speaking German with a Viennese accent, which would enable us to leave the reception camp, thus making space for more children to be brought over from Germany—surely it made more sense to allocate these permits to children who were still in Germany, who were worse off than we were, in more urgent need of them. It required our signatures before this could be done, he said, and held up a sheaf of forms. We would all be guaranteed our entry permits before we reached the age of seventeen or in any case within two years, in keeping with the conditions of our English visas. And meanwhile we would all be given places on *hachsharah.*

We had stood listening in silence and for a moment nobody said anything. Then we began to discuss the matter among ourselves, as if we believed that what we felt, or thought, or said could make any difference to what our leaders had already decided. We were given time for this before Teddy Kollek called for a volunteer to set an example.

Lise and I had been planning to go to the Land of Israel for almost three years, and for more than two months we had been counting on it. First it had been a question of getting the agreement of our parents—of our mother; our father left decisions concerning their daughters to her. Then we had needed to prove to the leaders of the selection camp that we were mature enough and of the kind to be an asset to the Jewish community in Palestine. We had directed our lives towards this aim as believers do theirs in the hope of getting into Paradise. And now we understood that we would not have deserved to go if, under the circumstances, we had insisted on it.

I found Lise's hand; we looked at each other and stepped forward.

"Sign here." She did. I did. Always more ready to come out with what was in both our minds, I said, to that young man who looked as if he might have been a leader in the Hitler Youth, "We didn't leave our parents, we didn't leave Germany, to continue to live in exile."

He took my hand, shook it and said, "I, personally, guarantee that you will get to the Land of Israel."

Almost three decades later, I was to remind him of that promise, and he kept it.

It made life in Dovercourt more important to me, to know that it was the beginning of a longer stay in England. I, too, would have to get used to drinking tea with milk, to sleeping under blankets, to not giving a real answer when greeted with "How are you?"

Being the first to renounce our entry permits into the Promised Land made Lise and me known to people. There were some who pointedly turned their backs on us and others who asked us to explain why we had done it and then argued—all having also signed away their rights and feeling that not the leadership but we were responsible because we had left them no choice. But many now turned to us, especially to Lise, for help and advice with whatever problems they had.

Among the adult volunteer camp staff was Zippora, a kibbutznik who happened to be just then in England. She had black frizzy hair and bright blue eyes and was in her late twenties; of Russian parentage, she spoke neither English nor German but, apart from Hebrew of course, only Yiddish. It made her an outsider. She had been put in charge of the clothing store.

Zippora sought us out and, with patience and goodwill, we managed to converse, she speaking Yiddish and Lise and I speaking German. We were enchanted to be in the presence of someone who had seen Lake Kinneret, and the Wailing Wall.

Among the donations which were the response of the British people to our arrival there was a vast quantity of clothing; it was known that we had left Germany with no more than we could carry. Zippora complained to us that, nevertheless, none of the children ever asked her for anything. Lise and I should come to the store and choose something. We answered that we had had enough of wearing cast-offs in Germany; if we needed to go on doing so then what was the good of having come to England? There were brand-new things as well, she assured us. To please her we went to look. From Balaclavas to Wellington boots, from vests to hair ribbons, whatever any child could possibly want was there, much of it straight from the manufacturers. We thought of our mother selling a pair of Meissen figurines she had cherished since her girlhood to enable her to buy us the windcheaters we needed—and how patiently, on her aching legs, she had come with us from shop to shop to find some that did not look like part of the Hitler Youth uniform. And even I, whose greed was a family joke, did not want to take anything.

We asked Zippora's opinion about what had happened at the meeting with Teddy Kollek. She said that once we children had left Dovercourt, no one would really care what became of us. And once we had begun to make our lives in England, we would be lost to the Zionist movement and maybe even to the Jewish people.

"But Zippora," we asked, appalled, "what can we do to make sure that that doesn't happen?"

All the Zionist children must be rallied together, she said. By this time all sorts of classes had begun to be organised, above all for the learning of English, but also in general knowledge and in some of the subjects—geography, history—teachers of which were among the volunteers. Children on their way to South America were meeting to improve their Spanish. We must organise Hebrew classes, Zippora urged us. Spare-time activities included community singing and ballroom dancing, under the guidance of the commandant, who managed the summer activities and had been recalled by the owners of the camp, together with the cooks and the cleaners, from his winter job. Learning to dance the Lambeth Walk, learning to sing "Daisy, Daisy"—was the way, Zippora asked, sounding more scornful in Yiddish, for people who took themselves seriously to spend their time?

If we were to organise a meeting, we asked her, would she attend and talk about the Land of Israel? She couldn't do that, she said: people would lose patience with trying to understand her; and, anyway, the staff had had to give an undertaking not to engage in political activities. We—meaning Lise and I—must manage without her.

Senta had a moral reservation: she was not going to the Land of Israel. Also, she belonged to the Bachad, one of the Orthodox parties; especially the communists, meaning mostly people from Vienna, would not come to a meeting if it were called by her.

Lise and I belong to the Maccabi Hatzair, a party which was, as we understood it, somewhat left of centre; the Jewish community in Bielefeld was too small for its Zionist children to have been given a choice. Because emigration was causing an increasing shortage of older children, we had both already had experience in leading groups.

Within ten days of our arrival—by the time the Christmas tree was put up—we held our first meeting. About twenty people attended. Nobody offered to take charge. Someone suggested that Lise should do it and all the others agreed. Lise, knowing how much I needed to see myself as her equal, said that she would take charge jointly with me. When I asked her, afterwards, why was it, did she think, that people had suggested her rather than me, or anyone else for that matter, she said that it must have been because she was known to be older. I needed to hear her say it. The truth was that Lise had—she still has—a talent for relating to people which at that time I envied in her. People liked her because of who she was; they did not like me and I believed that it would have been degrading to me to try to make them, I believed that it was shameful to want to be liked and was afraid that my wanting this would be found out. It gave other people power over me and I did not want them to know that they had that. Had I striven to be liked and succeeded I would still not have achieved equality with Lise: people's feelings went out to her without her doing anything.

We organised daily Hebrew classes and almost daily meetings, and before long all the Zionist children attended them. I had plenty of ideas; I told them to Lise and Lise put them to the group; from her they accepted suggestions which they would have rejected if they had been made by me. I did not mind this: it allowed me to believe that there was more to me than people realised and gave me a satisfaction the greater for being secret. It made me gloat, when I overheard someone commenting on the subject I had suggested for a debate, that it was better than anything Kate could have thought of.

We lacked books. Needing material about the Land of Israel, I began to write stories, and essays, and poems, and a whole sequence of "Letters from Jerusalem"; in my imagination I lived there. I did not want to be seen to monopolise the meetings, the group would not have tolerated it; I gave these things to other people to read out, saying that I had copied them from magazines and books. It was the only way to get them taken seriously; recognition mattered to me far less than that the thoughts of all of us should be occupied as much as possible with the Land of Israel.

Feeling so involved in what I thought was the most important activity in the camp, having the incentive to be writing, writing, I almost stopped feeling homesick and began to feel almost happy.

After the first chaotic days, we were made to sit, boys and girls separately, according to age, so that people who came to the camp, especially at weekends, with the intention of fostering one of us, could choose more easily: a boy of seven or a girl of ten—like that. My round face and naive eyes made Lise, in her emaciation, seem even older; more than once she was told off for sitting at my table and I had to explain that she was my sister and that I would not go anywhere without her. "Don't let her spoil your chances," I was told.

What chances? I, too, was already too old: it was rumoured that girls of our age would be taken only by people who wanted an unpaid servant; and for that, we believed, we might as well have stayed in Germany. The matter was not so simple: we—Lise and I and many others—wished to find guarantors for our parents, and there was no knowing whom we might meet once we had left Dovercourt. But knowing how desperately hard my father had been trying to arrange our emigration, as a family, for the past six years, I did not ever really believe that I stood a chance of succeeding where he had failed.

One day after lunch I was summoned over the loudspeakers to the office. I had not been aware that anyone had been looking at me; I had believed that it was written in my file that I was not available for fostering: not without Lise, or not at all because we were to go on *hachsharah.* But there they were, some British couple offering me a home.

I was told to shake hands with them and so I did. But if I looked up into their faces at all I did not look into their eyes. I had not confidence in the choice they had made on the strength of my appearance. Even Anne, who was miserly with praise, had once praised it: when I had paraded some garment she had said that I would look all right wearing a sack. Experience had taught me that, on closer acquaintance, people did not much like me. Supposing the couple were to reach the conclusion that they had made a mistake—then what would I do, then what would become of me? I had believed Zippora when she had said that once we had left Dovercourt no one would care.

My scant knowledge of English frustrated by my emotions, I said in German that I did not want to go with this couple, and the other people in the office—three members of the volunteer staff—all began talking at once: one saying how fine an opportunity I was being offered, one scolding me for being difficult, one appealing to my conscience, pointing out that by remaining in the camp I was stopping another child from coming to England.

If they would also take Lise . . . I said, weakening. If they had known me better they would have been unsurprised: it has always been part of my nature to ask for too much.

Not far from us was a smaller reception camp, for teenaged boys; they frequently walked over to us in the afternoons, under Dusch (short for Duschinsky). Dusch, also a refugee, was in his late twenties; he was good-looking in a Jewish way: dark eyes, dark hair, high forehead, and slightly curved nose. It was his gentle, caring manner which made him matter to me. He had a way of leaning forward as we talked. Perhaps it was his ear he was bringing closer because the hall was so noisy; but I saw it as a perhaps unconscious expression of his wish to get closer to me—of his mind to get closer to mine: I had read Freud and yet managed to remain naive about sex.

There must have been other occasions when he came over by himself; I remember only the one. The local cinema put on matinee showings especially for us; German cinemas had long been forbidden to Jews and most of us appreciated the treat. Not I: I had gone once, to see what I think may have been a comedy thriller, or more likely the programme consisted of two films which my memory has confused. I understood little of what was happening on the screen and less of the dialogue, and thought it not worth my attention, preferred what went on in my head. Also, I had hated the walk in the cold, and so this time I had stayed behind. Lise had gone, in a swarm of girls who had become her friends.

I had opened one of the fireguards and drawn my chair close to the stove. Footsteps echoing in the almost deserted hall made me look up: and there was Dusch, coming towards me.

He had not known that the others would all be at the cinema. "Lise as well?" he asked; it was an obvious question and

I thought nothing of it. "But now that I've come I'll stay for a while and we can talk," he said, and got himself a chair to sit down beside me. He asked who was so important to me that rather than go to the cinema I was writing a letter.

"It isn't a letter," I told him.

I needed someone with whom to discuss my problem. Talented children were being encouraged to come forward: private people and schools were offering patronage. You could demonstrate it if you were musical or could draw or paint. But I could write only in German; I needed some adult, to whom the authorities would listen, to vouch for me. I don't know what I expected would come of it; I just could not bear to be so anonymous.

"So you write poems," Dusch said, looking at me with his head aslant; spoken softly in all that stillness, his words sounded caring. "I'd like to read some of them, sometime." I believed that he meant it; only the fact that, of whatever I had, I had no copies, prevented me from handing some poems over to him then and there.

He leant back in his chair, with his hands in his pockets, and, looking away from me, said, "But, you see, it is generally held that poems can be written only in the language to which one has been born."

Had it been said not by Dusch but a total stranger I would still have believed it: I was still at the stage of believing what adults said. And I thought, if only someone had told me this before: I would never have left Germany.

Local schoolchildren came to entertain us, a scout troupe came, professional entertainers came from London. Between Christmas and the New Year, we were promised a concert; we did not get music as we had expected, but variety acts, including one the joke of which was that half a dozen people pretended to have been shot, one after the other, each turning out to have been the wrong man. The fake gunshots made some children scream but not with laughter.

I saw "Underneath the Spreading Chestnut Tree" and "Ten Green Bottles"—since these were the songs we were being taught—as prime examples of British culture, and preferred our Hebrew love songs to our homeland. I thought ballroom dancing decadent and preferred dancing the hora. I suggested to our group that, as Zionists—dedicated people—we should keep away from the general camp entertainments, and was astonished to discover that most of the others enjoyed them. It made me feel an outsider even among people whom I had thought of as like-minded.

Lise argued that it was a good thing if people could forget their relations in the concentration camps, and politics generally, if coming to England turned us back into children. But Senta agreed with me.

I said to Senta that, supposing I were to remain in England, by the time I was thirty-one I would be more English than German because I would have lived for longer in England that I had done in Germany. "You will never be other than a Jew," she argued, "who happens to have been born in one country and happens to live in another. You won't belong."

This wish, this need to be at home where I lived, that was the essence of my Zionism.

But I felt that I also only happened to be a Jew; I hated having to be one. I had been exposed to the indoctrination to which my generation in Germany had been subjected; I, too, had been influenced by it, damaged: I could not stop myself—though I tried—from seeing the Jews as the Nazis saw them, as less than human.

There was something so wrong with my life, I felt, that I wished that I had not been born, that I wished myself dead. "What you see as wrong," Senta said, understanding that I could not explain, as Anne would have done, "is that you can't be what you want to be, and you don't want to be what you are. You need to learn to accept yourself as a Jew."

And, suddenly, I could see it for myself. "Are you Jewish by race or by religion?" was a question which we children had been asking each other for years. Now that I had left Germany, I would have to stop hankering after being a German. And if I had to be a Jew, then I must be as Jewish as I could, which meant keeping all the observances, doing everything that Jews were enjoined to do and not doing anything that was forbidden. Then I would be a Jew "with all my heart, and with all my soul, and with all my might." All or nothing suited my nature.

To my grandfather, being Jewish had been a grace. The Jewishness he had brought to our family life had been a grace to us, too. By becoming, as he had been, Orthodox, I was trying—though I was not aware of it at the time—to regain the emotional security of my childhood.

February 1939–December 1940

(Whittingehame)

Our arrival in Whittingehame made the front page of the *Scotsman.* There was a photograph of a long line of laughing girls with their arms on each other's shoulders, Lise in the middle and I displaced from her side by the dogma that blood-relationships must be subjugated to the good of the community.

An advance party of twenty refugee girls, under the supervision of two young refugee women, the paper told its readers, was now living in the stately home of the Balfour family, which had long stood empty, to get it ready for the arrival of another hundred refugee children, both boys and girls. They were here to prepare themselves for life in the homeland which had been promised to the Jewish people by the British Government in the Declaration issued in 1917 when Arthur Balfour was Foreign Secretary.

There is snow on the ground in the photograph: it was the middle of February. Between Christmas and the New Year, in the reception camp at Dovercourt, some of the older boys and girls, or perhaps only one couple, had been discovered in bed together. By the beginning of January all the girls had been removed to a separate camp on the south coast.

Our journey to Scotland had been broken by three days in London, for medical examinations and to show us the sights: Buckingham Palace, the Tower including the Crown Jewels, the Houses of Parliament. At the entrance to Westminster Abbey, we discovered that most of us had nothing with which to cover our heads, without which we were not going to be allowed in. While we stood there, wondering what to do, a procession went past; Senta drew my attention to it, surreptitiously: she thought it better that the others should not see it. The demonstration was in support of the unemployed. "Keep foreign children out while our own go hungry," one of the placards read; Senta translated it for me.

We were the guest of, were shepherded by three or four Jewish women of our mothers' generation. Most of us came from a milieu which had been like theirs until Hitler had come to power. We understood that they meant well and tried to appreciate what, not only to me, was on the whole an ordeal.

"We are going to live in a castle," I wrote on the postcard Lise and I sent to our parents from London. To us Zionists, Lord Balfour was the most important of all British Lords ever: how could his family home be anything less? As so often, expecting too much, I was disappointed. Called, modestly, Whittingehame House, a house it was, though a grand one, with huge rooms with high ceilings and tall windows; and it was surrounded by parkland.

On the ground floor, the ballroom, its gold and white walls hung all along with tall mirrors, became our synagogue. The huge library—all the shelves empty except for the simulated books on the secret door—became our assembly hall. The smaller room between, also with French windows giving on to the terrace, became our common room. We ate in the two wood-paneled rooms at the front of the house, one of which had a dumb-waiter to the kitchen in the basement. There were other, smaller rooms used as classrooms.

While we cleaned and scrubbed and polished, we lived in the wing which had been the servants' quarters. Later, all the girls' dormitories were on the second floor, while the boys filled both the first floor and the wing, which had only one storey. The headmaster's quarters were in the other wing, with the matron's quarters and the two sickrooms above it. The other adults occupied the small rooms (former dressing-rooms?) among the dormitories.

A *hachsharah* ought not to have had a headmaster and a matron. But some members of the committee responsible for us—Jewish businessmen living in Edinburgh, mostly—thought of the place as a school: a potential Jewish Eton, one of them called it. Later, when the house was full to capacity, about a third of the children were not Zionists, nor were the majority of the adults. But by that time the nature of the community had been shaped by our kibbutz ideals.

Having settled in for the foreseeable future, we asked our parents to forward some of our belongings; Lise's and mine were the first to arrive. They were tea-chest-sized crates containing those of our favourite books which had not been banned in Germany, and such things as straw hats and cotton shorts we had bought in our last weeks at home in preparation for going to the Land of Israel. The notification from the port authorities included a bill for handling charges, and, in case these were not paid promptly, the tariff for storage charges, and the threat that, if these were not paid within a certain time, the goods would be sold by auction.

The crates meant more to us than mere belongings; they had been packed by our mother: they stood for home.

By this time Dusch had arrived in Whittingehame with the first group of boys. We needed him to translate and explain the papers to us, and he put our problem to the next general assembly. The committee was allowing each of us sixpence a week pocket-money. It would be impossible for Lise and me to redeem our belongings. Soon other children would be confronted with the same problem.

He allowed time for discussion. When this did not produce a solution, he pointed it out to us: what we needed to do was to pool our pocket-money. All we wanted it for was to buy stamps for our letters home. The stamps would be paid for out of the communal fund. Once that was agreed he suggested that we elect a treasurer.

"Lise," said Anneliese, a small girl with big breasts, from Vienna, the most demanding of the several who were using Lise as a mother substitute. I thought the suggestion funny because Lise had not done well at school. But the others would have accepted it had Dusch not had other ideas.

As a self-governing community, constantly growing in numbers, he pointed out, we needed also other officials. Until now, the adults had decided what work needed to be done and we had volunteered for it; the moral pressure of the community, the need for its approval, had made all of us do our best. We should elect someone who would be responsible for the allocation of work.

This was going to be the key position in the community; we could all see that. "Lise," Anneliese said again, and clapped her hands over her mouth, giggling, embarrassed to have again been the first to speak.

"Any other nominations?" Dusch asked, looking round the circle. There were none; Lise was the obvious choice, not because she was among the eldest but because people felt that they could talk to her and because they trusted her judgment. We knew enough about democratic procedures for someone to second the nomination. She was elected by a unanimous show of hands.

Only then did someone suggest that we needed two people: a boy as well. We elected Avri, a tall blond boy from Vienna, with crippled feet; he had been born with them like that. It was said of him—with some exaggeration—that he could make any girl fall in love with him, and that when he grew tired of her—as always happened before long—any boy would be happy to succeed him: so much were the other boys influenced by his taste.

We elected, altogether, a council of eight. Nobody else wanted to organise our spare-time cultural activities, for which I had been making myself responsible since Dovercourt. Having been nominated by Lise, I was elected to continue to do that; no one actually voted against me, out of deference to Lise, but there were many abstentions.

I did not know why I was unpopular, but I knew that I was: as I had been at boarding school; as I had been before that in the various children's homes in which I had spent some weeks every summer since the age of eleven. I was nice-looking—according to my family better-looking even than Anne; I was intelligent: always top of my class. There was no shortage of boys who fell in love with me, though I rarely responded; it was part of my nature to fall in love with young men beyond my reach: teachers, youth leaders, for instance Dusch. Grown-ups sometimes criticised me for taking myself too seriously; other children accused me of having too high an opinion of myself. I was aware that I suffered from what was known among us as *Geltungsbedurfnis*—the need to be acknowledged as someone who mattered. It was also said that before you could expect other people to like you you needed to like yourself. I hated myself and did not feel anyone's equal and there was nothing I could do about it.

The first headmaster appointed by our committee did not last for a month. He was an elderly man, small, bald, a disciplinarian, who conceived his chief duty to be to keep boys and girls apart. We felt insulted by this: did he think that consorting *in public* would make us licentious, did he think that his rules could prevent us from being that supposing we felt like it? Erika, another of Lise's close friends, who was underdeveloped and wore her hair cut short, one day dressed in a shirt and shorts and in assembly sat among the boys. We could not stop laughing; the headmaster could not make himself heard. Naturally, he thought that we were laughing at him—and I suppose so we were. He left the next morning.

Mr. Maxwell was a brawny Scotsman, with a passion for astronomy. That we referred to him as Maxi implies that we felt some fondness for him, perhaps because he looked picturesque, always wearing a kilt, often appearing in full regalia. The first time he addressed us, he used as his interpreter Hugo, another boy who influenced the rest of us. Hugo spiced his translation with insulting references to Maxi in the broadest Viennese. And Maxi was delighted with the reception we gave his speech.

Neither of these headmasters was Jewish, or knew even a little German, or had any understanding of us either as individuals or as a community. Dusch, who was trying to act as mediator, was blamed for what Maxi saw as our insubordination—our insistence on self-government—and the committee asked Dusch to leave.

Half of us worked in the mornings—in the house and on the home farm—and half in the afternoons, all spending some hours each day having lessons in English, in Hebrew, in general knowledge, and, as in Dovercourt, in any subject some adult there happened to be qualified to teach. (Maxi taught the senior English class astronomy.) Most of what spare time we had was spent in communal activities: general assemblies, public debates, sport, making music, sing-songs, and dancing the hora. Therefore, Dusch had got Maxi's permission for the members of the council to stay up beyond the general bedtime. On most nights we met in his room, and, after completing our business, remained to talk until midnight, at which time Dusch needed to rouse the bed-wetters.

As his parting gift to us eight he suggested an outing to the coast, on the first day of Shavuot (Pentecost), which—apart from essential work—would be a holiday for the whole community. No one else was to come or even to know of it until after we had set out.

I nearly did not go: and the consequences of that would have made a difference to the development of my character, to my whole life. As an Orthodox Jew, one needed to turn one's pockets out over running water, symbolically discarding sin. It need not be done until the second day, Senta whispered, when I reminded her of it, after she woke me even before it was dawn. Lise and Dusch had got up even earlier and were in the kitchen, preparing a picnic. I could not bear the thought of being left out.

The grounds of Whittingehame House were extensive. On the opposite hillside, across a valley, was a tower, a much more romantic building, said once to have housed Mary, Queen of Scots. Its ground floor became our laundry. Much further away, in the forest, was a large natural lake. We had been forbidden to leave the grounds; we had not had the leisure to do so until this excursion, which became known in the history of the community as "the bigheads' outing."

I had had my first real boyfriend—one who kissed me—at the age of thirteen and a half, at boarding school. Lise had not had one until now. Erich, another Viennese, dark-skinned, dark-haired, with dark, charismatic eyes, was younger and shorter than she; he was also on the council and it was obvious to us all, that morning, that those two were in love with each other. They lagged behind. Dusch tucked my arm into his and made conversation; I had no idea then that what he valued me for was being Lise's sister.

It gave me a magnificent illusion of freedom, of owning the world, to be striding out into the purple dawn; the night receded to grant us a cloudless sky.

When, after walking for an hour or so, we came out onto the main road, one signpost pointing to Haddington and the other to Dunbar, Dusch also did not know which direction to take in order to reach the sea. We turned at random, looking for a public telephone box from which Dusch could ring Maxi to ask him the way. He told us that that was why he wanted to ring him; but perhaps he was having second thoughts about what we were doing.

When the other children had discovered our defection, they had rioted: broken into the larder and feasted off its shelves. As if to emphasise their equal worth, they had refrained from causing any real damage. But Maxi felt them to be beyond his control: he ordered Dusch to return with us, at once.

We were received back with sneers and jeers. No cooking was done on Shabbat and on holy days; on this day, at lunch-time, people helped themselves to what prepared food was left and, ostracising the members of the council, ate sitting in haphazard groups on the lawn. And then called a general assembly.

I could not bear so much hostility and wanted to resign. Before the meeting, I said so to Lise; she told me that she had also thought of it, but that Erich and others were against it, and that it was necessary for us all to adopt the same attitude. I spoke to Senta and she said that resigning would amount to an admission of guilt and that the way to deal with the situation was to convince the rest of the community that we had not done anything wrong. I lacked the courage to act on my own.

The meeting was chaired jointly by people who had until then not made their presence in the community felt. They called for a vote of "no confidence" in the council. Dusch insisted that, first, he should be allowed to speak, and took all the blame. Nevertheless, the assembly voted us out of office and called for new elections. Against previous practice, voting was by secret ballot. Every single person voted for Lise; the rest of the councilors were also re-elected, though with a reduced majority—with the exception of myself. I received only a handful of votes: one from myself, one from Lise; one of the others must have been from Senta.

Recently, someone who came to Whittingehame only later said to me, "You—I remember you as a recluse."

Lise shared a room with Anneliese, and two other girls, one of whom worshipped her; all of us, including the girl herself, were too ignorant to realise that she was probably a lesbian.

When we had moved from the servants' wing up to the second floor, I had—being at that time still interested in having friends—chosen to sleep in the biggest of the dormitories, which held twelve beds. Just inside the door were man-high, white-painted wooden partitions; the one on the right provided hanging space for our clothes, the one on the left was fitted with shelves. I took a stool in there, pushed a pile of underwear aside: and had somewhere to sit and write.

Of course my hiding-place was discovered, and someone found out what I was doing in there. One day, I walked into the common room and there was Hugo, with a sheaf of my poems, reading one of them out so as to make people laugh. "Sorrow has got into my bones" was a quotation with which I was from then on, for some time to come, greeted by sundry people whenever they saw me.

There were at the end of our corridor, above the matron's quarters, several attic rooms which were not in use. I took an orange box—serving in those days as furniture in the kibbutzim—into the east-facing attic, and used the wide sill of the dormer-window as my desk. I got into the habit of getting up early, before anyone else was awake, to write, first by candlelight and then by the light of the dawn. This was when I willfully made my handwriting such that only I could read it.

I wrote a book-length poem about the return of the prophet Jeremiah; as he had once predicted the fall of Jerusalem, he was now predicting the catastrophe which was to befall the Jews of Germany. I had known of the existence of the concentration camps since the November pogrom; but though my adolescent imagination was fairly morbid, it anticipated no more than the margins of the Holocaust.

On June 27, 1939, Lise reached the age of seventeen. A fortnight or so before then, she received a letter from the Jewish Agency in London, telling her that she was to be given an entry permit into Palestine.

White-faced and trembling, she came to show it to me. "You can't go without me," I said.

She did not want to leave Whittingehame, the fine house and the marvelous landscape; of course she was happy where so many people had so much love for her. She probably did not want to leave Erich more than she did not want to leave me, but she did not allow me to know this. It was to be half a century before I found out—she did not mean to tell me but then let it slip—that on the morning of our departure our mother had made her promise her that she would look after me. As she had done almost since the day I was born.

I said, "I'll write to Dusch, he must get them to give me an entry permit as well." I believed that he knew how I felt about him, and that he did not feel the same way about me—did not allow me to know that he did—only because it was forbidden to him, as a youth leader, to become emotionally involved with a girl in his charge.

Lise, brightening, said, "That's a good idea. I'll write to him, too, he must help us. *Er hat mich doch lieb*" (After all, he loves me).

(When we girls had been there by ourselves, we had, for our amusement, drawn up a list rating our appearances according to communal opinion; I had come near the top and Lise near the bottom. When they learned of this, Avri and Hugo also made a list, in which Lise was among the first and I well below her: they had rated us according to our sex appeal. I had grown up thinking of Lise as, by comparison with Anne and me, ugly; it was her emaciation which was ugly, and her Jewish nose. Nevertheless, I believe that what attracted boys to her was not so much her physical self as her character which shone through it.)

It seems unlikely that the letters we wrote to Dusch were what brought him back. He probably had no work permit and was in need of bed and board. Maxi—or the committee—did not allow him to stay for long. Feeling that he had made use of me as a stepping-stone to Lise, I refused to have anything more to do with him, though I knew that this mattered less to him than it did to me: I could not look at him without longing, without tears coming into my eyes.

He told Lise that she had no choice: she had to leave England, as this had been a condition of her entry visa, and that all the available permits for Palestine were needed by others who were in the same position. If she were to remain until the following year, when it would be my turn to receive a permit, she would be too old for Youth Aliyah and then it would be I who would have to go without her.

She would have to leave and next year I should follow.

On her final evening in Whittingehame, the girls were queuing up outside the door of her room—its other occupants keeping out—for one last conversation. I caught her in the corridor on her way to having a pee; we gripped hold of each other and she said that she needed to keep her promise that she would speak with them all. I was too proud to ask her, and what about me?

On duty on our floor that evening was Ruth, who was not much older than we, and also a refugee and also a Zionist. When she tried to chase the girls away from outside Lise's door, they pleaded for a later bedtime and everyone else joined in: this was a special occasion: it was the first time that one of us was leaving for the Land of Israel. She conceded an extra half hour.

Then, with girls still besieging her, Lise sought me out, gripped my hand and drew me along to find Ruth; we met her in the corridor, by the gilded railings overlooking the wide stair-well. Would she give us permission, Lise asked, to take our bedding into one of the empty attics, to spend a last night together?

Perhaps Ruth was jealous of Lise for being so popular. She said to her, "If you had been less concerned with making yourself important to so many people, you would have had time enough for your little sister without talking all night." I thought, Ruth is right; but then she turned to me. "And if you weren't always scribbling and made more effort to join in, you'd have friends and not need your sister. In any case you are wasting your time, what the kibbutzim need is not poets but people who'll plant potatoes." And then she told us to go to bed, in our own beds as always. And left us standing there.

Knowing what mattered most to me, Lise said, "Ruth doesn't know. Ruth is prejudiced against all the arts, her father is a failed painter."

But I was still at the stage of believing what youth leaders told me. I thought that if going to the Land of Israel would stop me from being a writer, then I would not go there. I knew that it was too late to prevent Lise from going. That I did not tell her of the decision I had just reached was the first adult act of my life.

Years later, she was to say to me that she needed to leave me so as to be able to develop her own personality. But if I had dominated her—until we came to England, or perhaps only until I had left home for boarding school—it was she who had conditioned me to do so. All I understood at the time was that I would not have been capable of doing the leaving. Because she was able to do it, she was the one whom I saw as responsible for our separation.

I had not minded—until that last evening—that she had expended so much of herself on others; she had been there for me whenever I needed her and this had made me take her availability for granted. I felt that, of all the separations I had to endure, this one was the worst, but perhaps only because it came in addition to all the others. The only way I could cope with it was to believe that she was no loss to me: in self-defense I had to stop loving her.

Since I alone was her sister, and everybody would be saying good-bye to her, I decided to mark our special relationship by *not* saying good-bye. I got up before dawn, as on any other day, and sat at my window anaesthetising myself with poetry, while the sun rose, blood-red.

On fine summer mornings the roll-call was held on the wide gravel drive in front of the house. Lise, appearing for it, was greeted with cheering sufficient to make her weep. I was there, standing with the girls of my dormitory, while she was allowed to stand with whoever was taking the roll-call. It symbolised the unacknowledged truth: that she had from the first belonged with the adult leadership.

The lorry which was to take her to the nearest railway station arrived after breakfast. Before it was due, I ran away from the house, to hide behind the rhododendrons bordering the lawn. I was still sufficiently close to hear Lise calling my name; I could hear it being echoed by others. Now I wonder if I believed that by my refusal to say good-bye to her I could make her refuse to leave.

But in the days when we had lived at home with our parents, she had been known among us as "die gute Lise" (the good . . .), because unlike Anne and unlike me, she did not ever cause problems. It had been decreed, by people who had other priorities than we, that she must get on that lorry to catch that train, and so she did.

So she did.

With Lise gone and Senta away (she was too old for our community and spent much of that summer staying with an aunt), no one in Whittingehame remembered my sixteenth birthday. To have mentioned it would, in my opinion, have made the congratulations worthless. We were still getting dressed when I heard my name being called. Someone came to tell me that Batya wanted to see me. Batya had replaced Lise as the councilor in charge of the girls' work roster. She was not someone to whom I had ever given any thought. But as I hurried to her, still buttoning my blouse, I thought: there, she deserves her position. But she only wanted my advice about her knitting.

Senta was there in the week before war broke out. Her parents and her little sister were still in Hamburg, delayed by the problems the Nazis were causing them over the export of their belongings. Senta sent them a telegram saying that they should abandon everything and just *leave.* That is the final memory I have of her.

I, too, sent a telegram that week: to Anne, who had come to England in the spring and was now on *hachsharah* south of London. Our mother had repeatedly said that when war broke out—neither she nor our father believed that it could be avoided—she would kill herself. I asked Anne to telephone me because I needed to hear her say that she did not believe that our mother had meant it. Though I sent it in English, the message arrived garbled; both she and I waited by the telephone all that evening, each expecting the other to make the call.

At the beginning of the year I had corresponded—I once counted it up—with thirty-two people: some whom I had met in Dovercourt, some from Bielefeld and either still there or now scattered all over the world, and Marianne, my room-mate at boarding school and also a maverick. Perhaps only she and none of the others was my friend; they were merely people with whom to exchange opinion, more important to us at that time than the transient realities of our lives. But by that autumn I was corresponding only with my parents and with Anne.

After Lise and I had been severed I cast her out of my mind. I knew from my correspondence with my parents what the emotional cost was of exchanging letters with those I was not yet mature enough to do without. I hated receiving my parents' letters, barely read them, but felt that it was my duty to write back. Not writing to Lise was the only way I had of punishing her for having left me.

Anne had neither left me nor sent me away, and I was used to there being a distance between us even when we were together. It amazed and delighted me that she should take time off from her life in order to write to me. Her letters did not tell me much and were not long; they were proof that I mattered to her at least a little and that was enough for her to concede and for me to receive.

It was my mother who wrote to me; my father never added more than a few words, or even only his signature. He must have done so to let me know that he was all right—not killed, not arrested—but at the time this did not occur to me. I used to think that if that was all he was willing to let me have then his writing nothing at all would have been better. In spite of my telegram to Anne—with which I was merely dramatising my circumstances—I was not really worried about my parents; I would have said—but I would never have actually said such a thing even had I had someone to whom to say it—that I did not care what became of them. It was the only way I had of coping with the fact that there was nothing whatsoever I could do for them. And what was so hurtful about receiving my mother's letters was that they stood for her abundant love, which I still needed so much and was inaccessible to me.

By the time war broke out Whittingehame House had been filled to capacity, with 120 youngsters and, at any one time, between 15 and 20 adults. Almost none of the children who had come had left; even the few who were lucky enough to be followed to England by their parents were not thereby guaranteed a home. The staff, both Jewish refugees and Gentile Britons, was constantly changing. That autumn, Maxi left and we finally got the headmaster we believed we deserved: Bernard Cherrick, a Jew, a Zionist, an enlightened rabbi, who was to become the vice-chancellor of the Hebrew University of Jerusalem.

Also that autumn, there arrived a group of six young men; not old enough to be counted as staff but older than we were, they were known as the trainees. They were experienced youth leaders belonging to various Zionist parties, including the communist and the Orthodox ones.

As always when newcomers were expected, their coming stirred up the community: it was like a window opening to a fresh view. Some of the Viennese knew the two trainees who came from Vienna; the Orthodox one, from Hamburg, was also already known to a few people. "You'll fall in love with him," someone predicted for me; it was said that he had been orphaned as a baby and that his nickname, Pummi, derived from his aunt always cosseting him so.

I saw him for the first time in the basement corridor: I was going towards the kitchen and he, with another trainee, had come in from the yard and was going towards the stairs. Each having already been treated to gossip about the other, we looked back, both at the same moment. He was small for a man, no taller than I, was slightly built, with a pale, truly heart-shaped face, and a sweet smile. What was most special about him was that he had laughing eyes, deep-brown eyes that looked to me as if he were constantly sharing a joke with God.

From then on I no longer was—as I had been since Lise had left me—desperate to get away from Whittingehame; I no longer felt that being there was preventing me from getting on with my life. Instead of keeping out of people's way I now invented excuses for passing wherever I expected Pummi to be, just so as to catch sight of him, just so as to subject myself to the sensation which felt as if someone were fingering my heart.

My idea of torture was to be made fun of; when Pummi looked at me with his laughing eyes, I believed that he was laughing at me—that he knew how I felt about him and thought it something to laugh at. And because his existence made me feel more alive, I did not mind him doing that.

Not for a moment did I expect him to feel the same way about me, the social reject, the maverick, misfit. Not even when, without apparent reason, I was moved from the social group to which I had until then belonged to the one for which he was responsible.

Rather, I saw my transfer as a rejection by my old group. When Pummi asked us, at the first meeting I attended, for suggestions of what to read together on the coming Shabbat afternoon—when there was little else our Orthodoxy permitted us to do—eager to prove myself an asset, I volunteered to bring one of my stories. He looked extremely dubious about it, until some of the others reassured him: my ability to write was recognised as much as my inability to relate to people for their sake instead of only for my own. I was continuing to contribute to the wall newspaper which Hugo and I had founded; I now did so anonymously, but after almost a year people recognised my work as mine.

One evening, one of the trainees—a small, fat, already balding man from Prague called Otto—asked to speak with me. It was raining; there was nowhere to sit where we would not have been overheard, and so we walked up and down the ground-floor corridor. Otto was a toucher; he laid his fat warm hand on my shoulder, and later his fingers crept under my hair, to knead my neck. I was too interested in what he was telling me to be willing to risk offending him by objecting.

At the last meeting of the trainees, he said, Pummi had told them that he had fallen in love. He knew that this was in contravention of the rules and promised beforehand to accept their advice. He was the youngest of them, not yet twenty, and they all, Otto said, felt responsible for him and wanted him to be happy. So they had told him that he could let the relationship develop provided it could be kept secret.

I was wondering whom Pummi could be in love with, to whom I was sufficiently close for Otto to have chosen me as the go-between.

After the meeting, Otto said, Pummi had taken him aside and confessed that the situation was new to him and he did not know what to do next. And Otto, who did not want him to get hurt, had offered to find out. . . .

"I'll ask her," I said. "Who is she?"

The misunderstanding wasn't a joke to me. Though brief, it had hurt. I shook Otto's hand off and asked him, did he know where Pummi was now? Waiting, he told me, in the room he shared with Barry.

I ran upstairs. I had been on the afternoon shift in the kitchen and was still in my work clothes. Should I change before going to him? Or at least comb my hair? But I knew what it felt like to be uncertain and did not want to keep him waiting any longer. I thought that only superficial people loved one another for their looks, and that I wanted Pummi to love me for who I was.

Of course I knew which room was his but I had not been inside it since he had moved in. The beds stood on either side, against the walls between the door and the window; they did not leave much space. Pummi was lying on his, his head towards the door so that we saw each other's face upside down. "You look funny like that," he said, his eyes laughing not at me but with me.

Barry was sitting in an armchair by the window. He made no move to leave. Now I think that Pummi must have asked him to be there, and to remain if I were to come, because he feared the two of us being alone.

Some of us had relations in neutral countries who could forward letters to and from their parents. I lost contact with mine, briefly: until Anne was interned as an enemy alien living near the south coast.

One Sunday morning in the middle of May we were suddenly summoned to an assembly; so little had the war affected us until then that we did not make the connection as we wondered what was wrong. Once, we had been summoned unexpectedly for immunisation, when there was an outbreak of diphtheria; once we had been kept standing for hours while the staff searched the dormitories: a pair of shoes was missing from the store; one of the boys had sent it to his sister somewhere in England.

A policeman read out the names of about thirty boys. We failed to guess what they had in common which they did not have in common with the rest: that they were German nationals over the age of sixteen. Including Pummi. They were given an hour's grace.

Their girlfriends were told that instead of returning to their work they should help them pack. But Pummi wasn't supposed to have a girlfriend. When he wanted to go for a walk with me, he always took other members of the group along; he held hands with other girls as well as with me. That, and dancing the hora side by side with our arms about each other's shoulders was the extent of touching which he considered allowed, and someone would always before long break into the circle between us: I wasn't the only girl whose idea of bliss was to be close to Pummi.

That Sunday morning I was on duty in the kitchen. I preferred to work there, not because I liked cooking—I didn't—but because it gave me the feeling of being at the centre of things. (Perhaps because in my last years at home the family had lived mostly in the kitchen?) When the cook saw me, she asked, "Why aren't you with Pummi?"

I had had no idea that anyone knew about our friendship or even suspected it. Because of the way I saw myself I assumed that no one would think me a likely girl to have been chosen by Pummi, the most popular of the trainees in spite of his Orthodoxy—which in everyone else was considered by the non-Orthodox majority to be a subject for jokes.

If people knew about us anyway, I thought, then why should I not go to him? I wanted to, but was not sure that he would welcome me. When we were apart—for most of the time—I could half believe that he loved me; but in his presence I always thought that what he felt for me was no more than affection. Which he felt for everybody, just like Lise.

"Go!" they said to me in the kitchen. "Go quickly, you have less than an hour!"

I knew how the other couples would be spending the time: hugging and kissing. As I went up the stairs, slowly, I was hoping that the drama of the moment would serve to overcome even Pummi's reserve.

He was standing in front of a small suitcase open on his bed. He looked up from it as I came in and when he saw who it was, he asked, "How many shirts do you think I shall need?" As if we were long married.

Apart from our boys playing football against the East Linton village team, we had little contact with the local population. Now there was an air force camp nearby; some airmen began to visit us, court our girls. On their training flights, they passed low over the house, tipping a wing in greeting. Their commander forbade them to do it: it was dangerous, because of the surrounding trees. But they went on doing it.

On Shavuot—when the previous year we had gone on "the bigheads' outing"—being without Lise, without Senta, and now also without Pummi, I went for a walk by myself. It was again a warm, totally sunny day, and I found a hollow in a meadow to lie in while I made a poem. I always made them in my head and did not write anything down until I had finished with it. I left the place to go down to the stream in order to comply with the observance of turning my pockets out over running water.

I had done it and was walking along the valley, back towards the house, when I heard an aeroplane, or rather, I became aware that the sound of the plane which I had been hearing had suddenly ceased. And then I saw the smoke rising above the trees.

Others got there before me. The plane was burning vigorously and there was nothing to be done for the pilot still strapped into his seat. There was a gash in the meadow where a wing had first touched the ground: across the hollow in which I had lain.

I did not know what to do with this knowledge, I told it to no one. No one would have believed me; I didn't altogether believe it myself. In spite of the accusation against me that my inferiority complex made me arrogant—having read Freud, that was how we put it—I could not believe that I was so important to God. I would have heard, seen the plane coming and got out of the way. Had I been there, I might have saved the pilot. The thought of divine intervention in my life scared me so much that I did not want to believe it.

The event marked the beginning of the end of my relationship with the God of my fathers, the God of my childhood, who had personally created me as I was, knew me even to my soul, and determined what happened to me.

If what God there may be was not like an eternal father then there was no point in trying to relate to him, no point in praying. But I continued to attend all the services held by the Orthodox section of the community, and to keep all the observances, for the sake of the sense of belonging this gave me, and because I did not know what else to do. I could not write about it to Pummi, who had his internment to cope with, and I did not want anyone else to write about it to him. It was apparent to me that having lost my faith also meant losing this special relationship and I could not have coped just then with this loss in addition to all the others.

In June or July—I don't remember—we were notified that entry permits into the Land of Israel were being made available by the British Government to those of us for whom no other arrangements for their emigration could be made. All we Zionists, hugely delighted, exclaimed to each other, "Get rid of the lot!" echoing the slogan "Intern the lot" which had so hurt us. "You've got to show understanding for the position of this country, fighting alone against Hitler," the adults told us, to which we answered, "How about the politicians showing some understanding of us?" We thought that if the Germans were to arrive, they would thank the British for having already rounded up so many of the Jewish and the political refugees. Now we worried that our internees might not be released in time to travel with us.

Those most skilled in photography took passport photographs, with borrowed cameras; as aliens we had had to give up our own. The carpenters among the boys got busy making boxes for our belongings. Bales of pyjama cloth arrived, and the girls best at it spent their days cutting out and at the sewing machines. During the past year, we had all been provided with various items of clothing, dungarees for instance, and the girls each with navy blue material to make a skirt and blue or red checked gingham to make a blouse. The skirt I had brought from home still fit me: when I left my mother I stopped growing. The two cotton frocks we had bought for me with the eastern sun in mind had become too tight for my budding breasts before I had had the chance to wear them. I got up, as I was used to doing, before dawn, but now I went down to the sewing room, to use the material of the dresses to make blouses. Suddenly, briefly, I became popular among the girls who needed me to show them how to do this.

Lise had travelled by train across France and from Marseille by ship. Now, looking at the map, I wonder what route we had been intended to take. I remember only that we were kept waiting for transit visas by some country we were meant to travel through. By the time our boys were released from internment, before my seventeenth birthday at the end of August, the idea of our leaving England just then had been abandoned.

January–May 1941

(Whittingehame–Nanclwyd Lodge)

That summer, my second in England and the first of the war, a visitor to Whittingehame brought me greetings from a young man from home who was now also in England. We were distantly related, less to each other than through other people: his uncles and aunts in Bielefeld were my uncles and aunts too; my parents were his Onkel Paul and Tante Selma.

His father was not Jewish; Walter was uncircumcised and had been baptised. His hair was dark blond and though his eyes were brown, he could have chosen to pass as an Aryan but identified with the Jews. My parents thought well of him. My father had got him an apprenticeship as a bricklayer—under the circumstances of more value than a place at university. My mother praised the behaviour towards his aunt with whom he was living: better, she said, than that of many a son towards his mother.

He was five years older than I. We had spent much time together in our last summer at home: after he had lost his job and I had left boarding school. He was an atheist; an anti-Zionist, arguing that all nationalism was pernicious. He had fallen in love with me and I had been flattered; I had been unable to make up my mind whether or not I liked him.

On the day the synagogues burned he had been in Hamburg, meaning to take ship; he had previously worked his passage to Australia as a scullion, but had been thwarted in his intention to land there illegally. With his Aryan papers, he was safe in Hamburg, where nobody knew him; but he returned overnight to Bielefeld in case there was something he could do for his aunt and uncle, whose flat had been above the community rooms next to the synagogue.

As far as I knew he was, apart from my sister Anne, my only relative in England, apart from Dusch the only other person known to me outside the Whittingehame community. His greetings had been to Lise as well and I wrote to tell him that she was now in Deganiah. He wrote back, enclosing a postcard-sized photograph, showing him as a private in the Pioneer Corps, so handsome that a girl who saw it mistook him for a film star. I had not remembered him as being so handsome.

He wrote that they were constantly moved about and that he had a small package in need of safe-keeping. Could he send it to me? Of course I wrote back that he could. It was marked, "To be opened only in the event of my death."

It shook me to see those words. My curiosity was aroused so much that I could not resist it. The package contained letters, each still in its envelope, from a cousin we shared who was now in the United States; they concerned her younger sister, also in England, who had had a nervous breakdown. Walter had visited her.

"It's as well that you know," he wrote in answer to my confession that I had opened the package. She did not know who he was and "in case anything happens to me, I want you to promise that you will look after her." I had never liked the girl, who was Anne's age. Only because I did not want Walter to think badly of me, I gave him my promise.

If he cared this much about Hanne, I thought, then what about me? She hadn't even known who he was—which couldn't have been very nice for him. "You'd get more out of visiting me," I wrote, having got the headmaster's permission to invite him.

The war had caused our visas to be amended, permitting us to remain in the country for the duration, and to take work for which no British labour was available. The fund established to maintain us in Whittingehame for two years was running low. We were given the choice of continuing on *hachsharah,* in small self-supporting communities, or of having employment and accommodation found for us among the British.

For girls this meant going into domestic service, and I still believed that if that was what I was going to do, then it would have been better if I had stayed with my parents. Unhappy as I was within the community, much as I wanted to get away from it, I could not face the prospect of leaving it on my own.

Since Pummi had returned from internment I had felt uneasy with him. I lacked the courage to tell him that I no longer believed in God—or at least not in the God in whom he believed; I did not even believe in Pummi enough to be honest with him in the hope that he might be able to help me to overcome my doubts. My constant dissimulation was spoiling the love I felt for him. Yet I needed him more than ever, or rather, what I needed was to be allowed to remain a member of the group which he led. I was convinced that no other group leaving Whittingehame would at that stage be willing to include me; I could not have put it to the test without betraying my apostasy.

We were going to Nanclwyd Lodge, near Ruthin, in North Wales. Pummi asked me to join his advance party, to do the housekeeping. I knew what it would mean, to belong from the start and to fill such a key position. But it would have meant giving up seeing Walter, at least for the time being. We did not know what our living conditions in Wales were going to be like; I could not have invited him to come there instead.

It wasn't Walter himself who was so important to me, it was what he stood for: Bielefeld, home. Also, that I was expecting him provided me with an acceptable excuse for not going with Pummi. It allowed me to remain for a little longer undecided about what to do next.

London was being bombed and Walter was among those who were digging the dead and the wounded out of the ruins. Twice, his leave was postponed. Then, early in January, I received a telegram saying that he was arriving, definitely, that Wednesday morning.

I was told to take off as much time as I wished during his visit; I was known as a willing worker. To make the clock go faster while I waited for him, I went to help in the kitchen. In mid-morning, I heard my name echoing through the basement; I ran up the stairs to the ground floor and there he was: an apparently older man in ill-fitting khaki, with a convict's haircut: a stranger.

He had worked until evening, travelled through the night, and walked the several miles from the nearest bus stop. I served him a late breakfast and showed him to his quarters. There must by then have been ample space in the house, but the matron had allocated to him a small self-contained flat in one of the outbuildings, and I had got it ready. Returning to the kitchen, mortified, I asked myself, this is for what I have given up going to Wales with Pummi?

In the afternoon, when he came back to the house, I was better prepared for the reality of him; he had slept and now at least looked familiar. There was no "at least" about it: his familiarity grabbed me by the heart and stirred up my whole being; it turned me back into the fifteen-year-old I had been when we had last been together.

In spite of the snow lying thick on the ground, the frost in the air, night falling, so as to be by ourselves we went for a walk. It was better so. The setting was magical. Walking, I did not need to look at him and before long it grew so dark that I could hardly see him. His voice had not changed; what was special about it was that I had last heard it at home. He told me of his adventures: he had crossed into Holland, illegally, and the border police had handed him back to the Nazis. He spoke at length of the rescue work he was doing in London. It made all my concerns seem trivial. And when it was my turn, the past two years seemed by comparison of little interest, to him, to me. Instead, I talked of home and when I said "Mutti" he knew who she was, knew her; he knew all my family, my home town, my whole background. It deceived me into believing that I was known to him as my family knew me. It was next best to coming home.

It would not be just to say that he took advantage of me, of my situation. He knew what he wanted and I didn't know what to think of anything. He was still, or again, in love with me, and I was homesick. My relationship with Pummi had aroused a physical hunger which it had left unsatisfied. It was a child's hunger: for having my hand held, my hair stroked, for chaste kisses. Lise could have satisfied it. But she, my mother, my father, Anne, all were somewhere else. Only Walter was there and so I let him, I made him stand in for them.

It was frightening to travel by myself. From Scotland, through England, into Wales—it was all England to me because the language was English; until then I had not heard it much and hardly at all spoken it. Being a German-speaker in wartime Britain was not as bad as being a Jewish child in prewar Germany; it felt to me worse than it was because here the hostility was unexpected and because for the sake of the position I was now in I had left my parents, it felt to me as if I were harvesting punishment for it.

Pummi had written to me, "You will like it here: there are fields and forests, the landscape is just like the one you were used to at home." It wasn't the landscape which mattered; it could not compensate for our living conditions. There was a shed with a bucket which served as a lavatory; our water came from an outside pump. We had no electricity. The community, when it was complete, consisted of eighteen boys and three girls, some members coming from Gwrych Castle—a place in many ways like Whittingehame—near Llandudno. The lodge had three rooms. We girls had bunk beds in one; four of the boys had their beds in another, which was also the room in which we prayed. Among the things provided by the people in London who were responsible for us was a Torah scroll, as we were beyond the reach of a synagogue; when it arrived we debated for days the propriety of sleeping with it in the room but in fact there was no choice. The rest of the boys, including Pummi, slept in a stable loft, former grooms' quarters. There was barely space for us all to be together in the room we lived in; we crowded on benches round the dining-table.

We had a coal range to cook on, in a kitchen so small that there was space in it only for one of us at a time. We also had two Primus stoves, for use first thing in the mornings. Keeping a kosher house under such conditions would have been so nearly impossible that we gave up meat, which in any case we could not afford to buy. Most of the boys worked for the farmer on whose land we were living; they were paid according to age and Marcus was only fourteen. Sigi, who worked in the village garage, earned the most. The pooled earnings were needed to cover all our living expenses, including those of us girls, who, keeping house, earned nothing.

My place in Pummi's advance party had been taken by Ruthie. With her and Sigi—they were to get married—I had long had the only sort of friendship I was capable of: the active element being provided by them. "Do you want to take over the housekeeping now you're here?" she asked me, surprising me with her belief in my ability to do so. I thought that by remaining behind in Whittingehame I had had a lucky escape. Escaping was what I began to think of even before I had unpacked my belongings.

We got up early, worked hard, ate frugally, and were constantly so exhausted that we spent much of our spare time sleeping. But our first priority, for the boys at least, was prayer. The next, for all of us, was communal debate. We spent whole evenings discussing whether every decision should be made by all of us, or whether it should be left to Ruthie to decide, for instance, what to put in the sandwiches of the boys who worked too far away to come back for lunch.

Ruthie took me along to introduce me to the village grocer. He spoke to her volubly, with a strong Welsh accent; even without this I would have understood little of what he was saying. He was urging her to lay in a stock of what tinned food could still be bought off the ration. Probably, she was the first Jew he had ever met; but he clearly did not believe her when she said that we could not afford it.

The local people were scandalised to discover, through our farmer, that boys as well as girls were sleeping in the lodge. But when I went for a walk alone with Pummi, on my first Shabbat afternoon there, he would not even let me hold his hand. What did it mean, that he was my boyfriend? I asked, thinking of Walter. He answered, "I don't want us to have intercourse until we are married, and I don't want to ask you to marry me until I'm twenty-one, because I don't want to have to ask my guardian for permission." He said it in English and I did not know all the words; had he used the German for "intercourse" I would still not have known what he meant.

His whole speech, the length of it even, was more than I had expected. I could not see why he—or anyone—should wish to have me as a wife. I did not want to get married; more than anything else I wanted to have a home again, but by that I meant: with my parents. I did not love Pummi enough to give up for his sake the chance of one day once again making my home with them.

Wanting to do something for me, Walter made me presents. While he was visiting in Whittingehame, he took me on the bus into Edinburgh. I had only my windcheater; he could not afford a winter coat so he bought me a raincoat. For three years it remained the only coat I had.

I was still reading German in Whittingehame; we had pooled our books and had a good library. Walter sent me *Gone with the Wind* and, for weeks and months, I read it, every word, not understanding more than half of them. And also not understanding that what I was reading was teaching me almost nothing about all I so urgently needed to know. The second book I read in English—Walter sent me—was *The Cloister and the Hearth.*

The difficulty I had with the language obscured the fact that it was set in a bygone age. I had no means of knowing to what extent contemporary England was and was not like that. I had no means of knowing to what extent contemporary English society differed from the one presented in *Pride and Prejudice,* which was the third book Walter sent me, through the reading of which I tried to outgrow being a refugee.

Dusch told me that if I let him know which I wanted he would send me sixpenny Penguin books, which were then something new; he was able to get them at a discount. Ashamed to admit that I did not know what to ask for, I ignored his offer.

I met him again that spring while I was in North Wales.

For Purim, that gayest of all—that only gay Jewish festival—the whole community was invited to Gwrych Castle, through those who had come from there by the friends they had left behind. As many people did during the war, we hitch-hiked, in pairs. Ruthie had asked Gila and me to buy a few things for our household, in Wrexham; as we stood on the outskirts with sundry small packages, in the pouring rain, a woman driver stopped and asked us, "You poor things, are you selling things?"

In Gwrych Castle, that evening, there was some sort of theatrical performance. During it, there ran through the darkened auditorium the whisper, "Dusch is here." I dashed out to look for him. In the unlit passage—there were tall narrow windows all along one wall, impossible to black out—I had a torch shone into my face, blinding me, and heard his voice—doubly familiar because I had missed him so—exclaiming, "It's you, it's really you!" which made me think that perhaps, perhaps, I had, after all, been wrong in thinking that he had valued me only as a stepping-stone to Lise.

He sat me down beside him in a deep window embrasure and, hurriedly, we exchanged some superficial news. There were other people there with whom he needed to speak. "Don't go away," he said, leaving me there. "I'll be back."

I waited, for so long that I began to believe that he had forgotten me. Everybody else went to bed, the whole castle fell silent. How would I ever find the mattress on the floor which had been allotted to me? That was not what I cared about.

A long way off, I heard footsteps. The closer they came the more my heart-beat was one with them. Before I could be certain that it was he, Dusch said, breathlessly—as if all the time he had been away from me he had been hurrying back—"I was afraid you'd have gone to bed by now." I found his hand, clutched it, too full for speaking with a mix of gratitude towards him and of a rare self-approbation, because he had remembered and come back to me. I could almost have thanked God, I was so gleeful to have been singled out for so much grace.

Sitting cosily close in the lightless stone window embrasure in the sleeping castle, whispering, created for me the illusion of utmost intimacy. The question of the existence of God and how to relate to him was as real a problem to me at that time as the separation from my parents, and one of greater urgency: as an unbeliever, I could not go on living in an Orthodox community. But where else could I go, what prospects did I have, what future even? I thought Dusch would know. I expected him to tell me what to do, I still needed to be told; I would have followed his advice if it had been something, anything other than what it was: that I should remain in Nanclwyd Lodge, for the foreseeable future.

I was not completely honest with him: did not tell him about Pummi or about Walter, because I did not want him to know that, believing myself—no: having discovered myself—to be not good enough for him, I had made do with lesser men, two of them, who together, in my opinion, amounted to less than he.

As I tried to explain my circumstances, to explain myself, I began to feel sorry for this girl, too young, too alone, to be in such a predicament. I wept for her, for myself. I wept to entice Dusch to comfort me.

Schiller, by the age of eighteen, had written *Die Räuber.* I was in my eighteenth year, and what had I achieved? A few poems, a few prose pieces, in a language which I needed to disown. My visit with Ruthie to the village grocer had made me realise that what the writer in me needed—no matter how much the girl shrunk from it—was contact with English-speakers; doing the shopping, Ruthie had learned more English within a few weeks than I had done in two and a quarter years.

Walter was also without a home, without resources; but he was male and old enough to be answerable to no one. I saw his being a soldier as granting him the freedom of the kingdom: on his next leave, towards the end of April, he visited me in North Wales. We had not the space to put him up; we could not afford to feed him. He stayed in Ruthin and daily came out on the bus. He stood about with his hands in his pockets, watching me, or sat reading a newspaper, while I did my share of the chores, and whenever possible took me off to lecture me. He had always responded scathingly to my interest in religion; now he was just as scathing about our communal way of life. He had no more idea than I had of what I should do; but he was convinced that I ought not to stay where I was and said so before I could tell him that I wanted to leave. I contradicted him, so that he would go on stating the case for my leaving until he had answered the least and the last of my doubts.

He could not be expected to know what was best for me; I knew that he wanted the best for me and I thought that that was the same thing. I knew that he felt responsible for me on my parents' behalf and this made me entrust myself to him.

Ruthie and Gila agreed to let me take a day off, on the understanding that they would also be able to take a day off, soon. Walter and I went walking, as we had done in Whittingehame.

It was the first really warm and sunny day of the year—or the first one I noticed. I returned to the grim little lodge with a sunburned face, having spent hours lying on my back on a hillside, with Walter on top of me. He was as aware as Pummi that one thing could lead to another; but he was more permissive before drawing the line: all my buttons remained done up, all my garments remained in place. Though I felt his erection against my thigh, I had no clear idea of what it was. Perhaps my mother, and Anne, and Lise, each had believed that one of the others would tell me the facts of life.

That Pummi, and Walter, wanted to marry me did not make me think more of myself but less of them: I always thought that anything within the reach of someone like me could not be worth having. I saw my leaving Nanclwyd Lodge not as a move to get away from Pummi so much as a move towards independence; it had to do with Walter only in as much as without him it would not have been possible for me to leave. Once I had made my decision, I wrote to Dusch, asking him for the loan of five pounds. I received no answer. Perhaps he had not got my letter; but pride forbade me to ask again in case he had.

Walter wrote to me frequently, now and then enclosing a ten shilling note and apologising for it not being more. I ought of course to have handed them over to the treasurer of our communal fund. But I didn't.

Almost every week, one of us girls went into Ruthin to buy things we needed which couldn't be got in the village. Dreading contact with strangers, I had more than once forgone my turn. So the other two had to let me go when I wished to do so. I went to the railway station, offered the three notes I had to the old man in the booking office, and asked him, "How far will this take me?" At least, this is what I meant to ask, with whatever English words I managed to stammer out.

The old man smiled at me kindly and kept me talking. Before long I felt a hand on my shoulder and looking round and up saw that it belonged to a policeman. The idea that I was—perhaps—being mistaken for a spy made me laugh: the Nazis would have known better than to send someone with such a minimal knowledge of English!

He was only a constable, and very young; after examining my identity papers he didn't know what to do with me, who was growing hysterical. He led me back into the town, to the police station, firmly gripping my left upper arm all the way. Having grown up in the presence of a rough police force, I did not dare to struggle.

I was questioned, gently, patiently, by an older (more senior?) policeman, who then explained to me, repeatedly, until he was certain that I had understood him, that in order to travel anywhere I first needed to get permission from the police of the place I wished to go to. As an afterthought, he asked me how I was earning my living and, after I had managed more or less to explain this, if I had registered with the local labour exchange. I hadn't; no one had told me that I needed to do that.

It seemed hardly worthwhile, as I would be leaving. But he had told me where to go and he had been so nice to me that I did not want to disobey him. At the labour exchange, I did not understand what I was being told about national insurance stamps, except that it had something to do with my "employer." Which meant that when I got back I needed to explain my visit to the labour exchange, at least to Pummi.

I was not averse to lying. I did not want my decision to leave to be subjected to communal discussion. Even writing to Dusch, I had feared that the committee responsible for us would hear of it and be able to stop me. But on second thought I felt that I owed it to Pummi to come out with the truth. Late that night, Marcus came back to the lodge to fetch some aspirins: Pummi had said that he had a stomach-ache and that that was why he was lying awake and weeping.

I told Ruthie—and Sigi—the truth, too: I thought that I owed it to her—and Gila—to give her the chance, before I left, to get a replacement for me from Gwrych Castle.

I had little idea of the geography of England and we had no map or atlas; had we owned either we would, as aliens, have needed to have handed them in to the police. Anne was at that time still interned on the Isle of Man; not wanting to be a burden to her, I did not ask her advice. I knew that Walter's unit, now building army camps, was being frequently moved; in any case I did not wish it to look to him—or to Pummi—as if I were leaving Nanclwyd Lodge for his sake. I had no reason for choosing as my destination one place rather than another. But I knew that several girls from Whittingehame—non-Zionists—had gone into domestic service in Leeds; I had heard it said that Leeds had a large Jewish community. On the other hand, on the train out of Germany, Lise and I had shared a compartment with two boys, the brothers Silberstein, also from Bielefeld, on their way to their uncle, who lived in Birmingham. So I knew that there was at least one Jewish family there.

I wrote two brief identical letters, therefore, one to the police in Leeds and one to the police in Birmingham, since now that my intention was becoming known I felt the need to leave with increasing urgency: and one of these places might refuse to have me. I decided that whichever was the first to grant me permission, that would be the one to which I would go. And if I did not have enough money to reach it by train, I would walk the rest of the way.

Perhaps I had wanted to keep my intention to leave a secret because I had not meant, not really, to carry it out: it helped me through the days to tell myself, each day, that if I wished I could make it my last one there. I did not want to be in Nanclwyd Lodge; but I did not want to have to go through the process of leaving: of once more putting a place and its people behind me, for the sake of making an end rather than for the sake of making a new beginning. What reasons, what single reason did I have for believing, for hoping even, that in Leeds or in Birmingham I would find it less difficult to live than I was finding it where I was, than I had found it in Whittingehame, in Dovercourt—than I had ever found it anywhere except at home in Bielefeld with my parents and sisters?

The letter from the police in Leeds, granting me permission to go there, arrived first. There was a bus to Ruthin at twenty minutes past one which stopped on demand almost opposite the lodge. One of the boys who came back for lunch was Dov; we had been together since Dovercourt and always disliked each other. That day, when he saw me ready to take the bus, he said to me, “Pummi told me that you’re going to Leeds, I have a brother there, would you take this letter?” He must have seen that I was annoyed: with Pummi, whom I had asked not to tell anyone; he said, “I didn’t say anything bad about you, I left it open so that you can see that I didn’t.”

There was no stamp on the envelope: only the name and address. I realised that it was better than having nothing. I almost snatched it, not wanting Dov to know that I was trembling. I was both sweating and trembling as I shook hands with those who were there: Ruthie, Gila, my replacement, half a dozen boys, including Pummi. Not he, not anyone, asked me to change my mind and stay. As I walked out, before I had shut the door they were going on with whatever they were doing. I stood waiting for the bus within view from one of the lodge windows, but no one there was interested in taking another look at me.

I was travelling light, with only my briefcase—which had made me feel so grown-up when I had carried it for the first time, two and a half years ago now, before leaving Bielefeld.

Besides the obvious necessities, it held an envelope of photographs from home, a furry white cat the size of my palm which had been a rare present from my father, and a book of sepia photographs recording the making of Tel Aviv, from the first meeting of the founding fathers in the sand dunes in 1908, to 1926 views of the thriving modern town. It was the one possession I had inherited from my grandfather. I would have valued as much keepsakes from my mother and my sisters but had none.

The rest of my belongings I left ready packed for forwarding once I had an address. But most of my papers—all that German poetry and prose—I burned, before setting out to turn myself into an English-writer. I also burned the letter I had received from Stefan Zweig, a German author whom I then revered; I had sent some of my writings to him, living in exile. He had commented, *So lange es noch junge Menschen wie Sie gibt, braucht einem um die Zukunft des jüdischen Volkes nicht bange zu sein* (As long as there exist youngsters like you, one need not fear for the future of the Jewish people). To have received this letter, to have cherished it, bothered me: as much as if I had come by it dishonestly.

I still believed that it was true, what I had argued in Dovercourt, that, supposing I were to be allowed to remain in England, then the day would come when I had lived there for longer than I had lived in Germany: and from then onward I would be more English than German.

May–December 1941

(Leeds)

Having enough money to pay for my ticket to Leeds—it left me with one ten shilling note and some change—did not make buying it simple. "Single?" I was asked by the booking-clerk, who was not the same old man. I had not expected to be asked something and did not know what he meant. He repeated his question, more loudly each time, twice. Then he put it in full and I knew the word "return." "I'm not coming back," I told him, upset to tears by the exchange of words: by needing to have it, by it being so difficult, and by the thought of setting out for the unknown.

There was no train until evening. The ticket inspector told me that I needed to change; he told me where. But every station was blacked out and all the name plates had been removed; from the announcements I learned no more than the number of syllables in any name, and was too ignorant to be able to guess where we were. But I knew from other people's conversation that we were outside Manchester when the train stopped, for a long time, because of an air-raid.

On arrival there I was told that I needed to change stations. Desperation overcame my diffidence and eventually, in the near darkness, in that press of strangers, all except me seemingly knowing how to reach their destinations, I found a guard who called out, loudly, "Anyone going to . . . ?" whatever the name of the other station was. A group of men took me along with them; we walked across bomb-sites, with searchlights sweeping the sky. I thought that they might be Jews but did not dare to speak for fear that they weren't and, hearing my German accent, would abandon me.

"Is this the train to Leeds?" Having asked once, I did not mind asking again as much as I minded still not being sure. It was one which had individual compartments, no corridor, such as I had not been in before. The guard whom I had asked shut my door; since it could not be opened from the inside I believed that, hearing my German accent, he had locked me in. All the way to Leeds, while the day and my new life were dawning, I feared that on arrival I would be unable to get out.

I expected people to react with hostility, partly because of the mass internment the previous year, and partly because I had had that experience, though not often; and perhaps sometimes it was merely my foreignness people were reacting to—by raising their voices and/or treating me as simple-minded. But chiefly, I think, I expected hostility because I had grown up in a hostile environment and feared every stranger, every strange place, every situation which was new to me.

I coped because I had to, with a constant earthquake within, its dust getting into my eyes. But when I had the choice, whether or not to buy myself a cup of tea that morning for instance, I did not bully myself; though I very much wanted one—I had had nothing to eat or drink since the previous lunch-time—I was being kinder to myself by going without. Even in such an everyday transaction there were too many pitfalls for me, who, in spite of the Nazis and perhaps even because of them, had had as the youngest of the family such a sheltered childhood. Leaving me unprepared for the solitary destitution into which my idiosyncrasies had pitched me.

I had chosen to travel overnight so as to have the whole day in which to find myself a bed for the following night. That was the thought in my mind as, wearing my English-made raincoat, carrying my entire material assets in my briefcase, I stepped out of the railway station into Leeds. I needed a bed for that night, more than I needed food and drink and sleep, or money, or luck, or love: more than I had ever before in all my seventeen and three-quarter years needed anything.

The letter which Dov had given me for his brother Peter stated that it was written at the request of his youth leader, meaning Pummi, and that the bearer, though she would not say so, was in need of help. He should take her to his housefather or some other responsible adult, and make sure that she was not simply turned away.

I don't remember the exact words: I found it hurtful to read and so did not read it more than once.

Peter turned out to be younger than Dov; he was perhaps twelve, and very much more likeable, or at least I found him so. He was a pupil at an ORT—vocational training—school which had been evacuated, staff and pupils, from I think Cologne; it was spread over four large houses in Chapeltown. I arrived there so early that the boys were still getting dressed.

I must have been in a vulnerable frame of mind; I wished that Peter had been older so that I could have fallen in love with him: he had large dark eyes dominating a face as sensitive as Pummi's. The housefather, who, though balding, was not really old, reminded me of my grandfather. He gave me what at the time I believed to be his own breakfast, of cocoa and a buttered roll both with the taste of home, and left me by myself in what must have been his own room, while he went about his duties. I had kept myself awake throughout the journey for fear of being carried past my stop; sitting in an armchair by a window looking on to roofs, I fell asleep.

I was woken by the housefather asking me if I was still hungry; placing just then too high a value on food, I didn't like to say that I was. He told me to go to the office of the Jewish Refugee Committee; he explained where it was. Wanting the being looked after to go on, and on, I could not listen and he decided to let the charming young Peter show me the way.

He had not understood the directions either. We wandered

through residential streets, all seemingly alike with brick-built terraced houses. Beside one gate was a polished brass plate with the words "Refuge Assurance." I misread them and thought that this was it: the place where refugees were reassured.

When we found the office, its atmosphere, and the man behind the desk reminded me of my father, who had for some years kept the books of our home community, and also had grey hair combed straight back, and such a full face, and brown eyes. Wanting this stranger to think well of me, to think about me, I realised, as I had not done until that moment, that I had made myself into a vagabond.

I had already told him my name, which would have meant something to any Bielefeld Jew but here meant nothing. Why had I come, he asked, in German, with my father's intonation (perhaps he was also a Berliner), if I did not want anything? I could not have asked him for something without weeping, and as much as if it mattered I did not want to weep in front of him. My address?

From behind my shoulder, Peter answered for me that I did not have one.

As my father would have done, not only for me but for all the people who came to him for advice, he solved easily what to me had seemed such a huge problem. He wrote down several addresses of refugee families looking for lodgers. In addition, he gave me three pound notes. I felt as grateful to him as if he had made sacrifices for me.

Peter went off to his lessons. Now knowing what I must do, I felt that I could move more freely on my own. By mid-morning, I had rented a room, paying a week's ten shillings in advance. From there I returned to the hostel and Peter's housefather, as I had been told by him to do.

He had meanwhile asked for and been given permission to engage me for two mornings a week; the boys cleaned their own rooms, but I was to clean the bathrooms and lavatories, passages and stairs. Within a few days, the same work was arranged for me in two other hostels, providing me with five mornings' employment, for which I was paid one pound, and in addition got my midday meal in the dining-room of the main house. Pleased with me, they were soon employing me full time, doubling my wages. I did not realise then how well they were paying me; I was not again to earn so much for years. I spent the afternoons at the various hostels, mainly washing socks by hand and cleaning windows.

One of the hostels was run by an elderly (to me) couple from Bielefeld; they knew my parents but had not been known to me. In one of my mother's last letters—Anne was about to be released from internment, having volunteered for the ATS—she wrote that she had heard that I had become Frau Wielenz's maid. From when I had suffered from the coldness of Dovercourt, my letters home had not been telling the whole truth, and more recently they had been full of lies. I did not want my parents to worry about me, and there was anyway nothing they could have done to help me. It angered, mortified me, that they should know that I had become a housemaid; I still believed that for that I might as well, I would have done better to have stayed in Germany. Their knowing that I was a housemaid seemed to me to be much worse than my being one.

I wasn't employed by Frau Wielenz, I wrote back, convinced that that made a difference because Frau Wielenz was also only a refugee; and to prove it to myself I refused to scrub the floor of her private bathroom, though she offered to pay me sixpence for it if I did.

If I had been keeping a diary during the next few weeks it would have included these entries:

— On Saturday I went into town to see what the money I am going to earn will buy me. Before long, the conductor told me to get off the tram. I asked why and he thought I was arguing and started to shout at me. I closed my ears for fear of hearing the word "Jew"—I was coming from Chapeltown and had already been told that this is a Jewish district. (On the morning of my arrival in Leeds I had been given a penny ticket; it took more tram-rides before I understood that this paid for only a short journey, except before seven o'clock in the morning.)

Because of what happened, and for fear of not recognizing my stop, I decided to walk back. I get lunch at the ORT only on working days. My hunger reminded me that I needed to buy food, for Sunday as well; Mrs. Rosen has been "lending" me my breakfast. Fearing that the shops would soon be closing, I made myself go into the first grocer's I came to after this, and tendered my ration-book, to register there. It was refused, the man behind the counter saying that I should go to the shop where my family are regular customers. I left in tears and discovered that I had been following the No. 2 tram route in the wrong direction, further and further away from Chapeltown.

— I had to queue at the labour exchange and when it was my turn, the clerk refused to deal with me. I didn't know the word "juvenile"—at first I thought that it had something to do with being Jewish.

— I wrote to Ruthie, asking her to forward my things. She wrote back that Gila, before leaving for London, unpacked them and took what she wanted and that she (Ruthie) doesn't have time just now to pack up again what is left. I have only what I brought with me and clothes rationing has just come in.

— I eat lunch at the ORT with the agricultural trainees, four young women. There is something wrong here: they are much more adult and self-assured than I, yet I am the one who is already earning her living.

— On Friday night (my second in Leeds) I went to the synagogue, not to pray but just so as to feel at home among Jews. All the melodies were different, so that I couldn't join in the singing, and it was worse feeling an outsider because I hadn't expected it. There wasn't the same atmosphere, either. The women sat separately; they all looked at me, but no one spoke to me or invited me home, as Jews are supposed to do with strangers—as Opa invited Papa and he fell in love with Mutti.

— Going to work in the mornings, when I pass people waiting at the bus and tram stops, I get such a look from some of the men! Is it because I wear an overall in the street? I think it is just like a summer frock and that it looks nice on me.

— I work almost without supervision, especially in the afternoons. There are lots of (German) books in the bedrooms and I spend my time reading instead of cleaning the windows. I borrowed a book, to finish it; I like it so much that I think I won't take it back. These boys are all better off than I am, living among their own, provided for and looked after.

— I wrote to Whittingehame for the addresses of the girls who went into domestic service here, and met with Irma and Ilse on their evening off, in a cinema cafe. I knew that I had nothing much in common with them; they are like the maids Mutti employed before Hitler came to power.

— When I called for Irma she was still getting ready: she had her hair in curlers and was painting her nails bright red. She put on silk stockings and high-heeled shoes and told me that I won't get a boyfriend unless I do the same.

— How does the couple who comes to play cards with the Rosens make love? She is no bigger than I am and he is a huge fat man with a protruding belly which must surely get in the way?

— When I told Ilse that I had never been inside an English home, she invited me for Sunday afternoon, with the promise to show me over the house. But her mistress didn't go out as expected. She (Ilse) got permission to give me "tea"—which she had meant to give me without permission. She asked me if I liked baked beans and when I told her that I didn't know what they were, she got us those, served on toast. They were delicious. Now I know what to get for my weekend meals.

— I met Ruthie in the street. I was so astonished when she told me that she has an aunt living here—that she let me go to Leeds without telling me this, while allowing me to believe that she was my friend—that I forgot to remind her to send on what is left of my belongings. (She never did.)

— The cook for Irma's household is a young Irish woman. She told us that she knew that she had married the wrong man and decided to leave him when they went dancing and there were other men in the hall whom she would rather have been with. Among the older boys at the ORT there are several whom I would prefer to Walter, Max for instance. But he told me that he is looking for an English girl whose parents will be like a mother and father to him.

— On Saturday and again on Sunday I went to the Roundhay Park. It was quite crowded. The weather was so nice that I stayed all day; I lay on the grass sunning myself, and incidentally saved on food.

It would be all right there if people didn't continually try to pick me up. I wouldn't mind this, in fact I would welcome it, if only there were a way of knowing something about a young man before entering into a conversation with him. How can I tell when they're all in uniform? I am sure that the sort of boy whom I would like would not try to pick up a girl! How can I prove that I'm a nice girl except by not allowing myself to be picked up? I can't even tell the difference between uneducated speech and a regional dialect.

— I was told of a hostel for young Germans and I went there. They are not Jewish, but either of Jewish descent or political refugees, and belong to the FDJ—Freie Deutsche Jugend (Free German Youth). They gave me a cyclostyled magazine brought out by their movement; I should like to contribute to it and shall start to attend their meetings.

— Herder, with whom all the agricultural trainees keep flirting—he eats at our table—invited me to a play put on by the Yiddish theatre company evacuated from London. In the audience I saw so many familiar faces that I felt almost at home.

— I was right to believe that once I was living among the English my knowledge of the language would quickly improve. I can now understand almost everything I read, and at least the gist of everything that is said. Talking is a different matter. Especially when I am being made to feel self-conscious about it, I stutter and stammer and cannot think of the words I want, worse than when I arrived in the country and still had self-confidence.

The first poem in the English language which made an impression on me was "The Force That Through the Green Fuse Drives the Flower." I read it in Whittingehame, in a copy of the *Horizon* magazine which was on the headmaster's desk when I was cleaning his study. That Chanukkah (Festival of Light) we were each given a Penguin book and one of the girls got an anthology of modern English poetry, with photographs of the poets, Dylan Thomas among them. She wouldn't exchange books with me but she let me borrow it.

Dylan Thomas made me fall in love with the English language.

I browsed in the bookshops in Leeds and discovered *Penguin New Writing*. I bought every issue; they were the first English books which I bought for myself. I read them from cover to cover, as the only way open to me of identifying with the writers. It is no exaggeration to say that I would have been willing to give my life to be one of them. John Lehmann invited contributions from newcomers; I had either read in the *New Statesman* or heard at the ORT that he was an infallible judge of burgeoning talent.

I had already begun to make poems in English, walking about the streets and the parks of Leeds. Pride forbade me to buy a dictionary. I wanted to learn the language as a child learns its mother tongue: with immediacy.

When I heard nothing from John Lehmann I told myself that my poems had probably not even been read, as they had been handwritten instead of typed as stipulated. But I knew what a liar I could be when it suited me, and drew the line at believing the lies I told myself.

I needed to write as I needed to breathe, and continuing to write also in German was my escape route: the one way still available to me of returning home. I sent these poems to *Die*

Zeit, the only German language paper I knew of with an editor in London. He did not publish them, but wrote that the reason for their rejection was lack of space. I was inclined to believe him because he invited me to call on him should I ever come to London.

I instantly decided that I would go there for this purpose. I wrote to Walter that I was saving up for it: in the hope that he would send me a contribution. He wrote, "There are a dozen writers in exile, many of international standing, for every article *Die Zeit* has the paper to print, you would be wasting your money." But I knew that his real reason for not wanting me to go to London was the bombing. He had lived through the reality of it, which I could not even imagine.

I would not have placed much value on being published in *Die Zeit,* seeing it as "only a German" paper. But I rather liked myself in the part of one travelling up to London for the purpose of an interview with its editor. The reason why my writing was so important to me was that in this one respect I did not feel inferior.

When I met Pummi again, almost fifty years later, in the kibbutz in Galilee which he helped to found, he reminded me that I used to write poems to him. I did not write poems to Walter: it was a different sort of relationship. Emotionally, it was akin to my relationship with Lise, to whom I have not written a poem in all my life; perhaps the explanation is that they loved me better than I loved them.

Unlike everyone else, including at this period my family, Walter knew practically everything about me; as I didn't care so much what he thought of me, my letters to him were more honest. As far as Anne was concerned, I always felt that I needed to live up to her. I did not feel that I needed to live up to Walter, or to Lise. If this implies that I did not think much of them, it may be true, but it didn't matter, because I thought even less of myself.

As I was waiting for him to come on leave late on a Wednesday afternoon sometime in July, I thought about what had been said by Annie, the Irish cook for Irma's household, and decided that I could not expect my boyfriend to be one whom I saw as better than anyone else—since I thought of myself as being inferior to almost everybody; I decided that Walter and I were about right for each other. My chief reservations about him were that he was also a refugee, also without resources, and only a private—at that time: he rose to sergeant—in the Pioneer Corps.

His best friend was Hai (short for Haimann), also a half-Jew, who had come to England with his Gentile girlfriend to get married—which they couldn't do in Germany because of the race laws; they had been caught here by the outbreak of the war. Walter wrote pointing out to me how much better off Clara—a "real" German—was than I, as the wife of a soldier. If we meant to get married, it made sense, he wrote, that we should not put it off: it would instantly do away with all the discrimination against me, free me from all the rules and regulations applying to enemy aliens, and in addition provide me with a soldier's wife's allowance so that I would not need to work unless I wanted to.

Perhaps I was still feeding on the abundant love I had stored up in my childhood. His must have been harder than mine; he did not talk about it, I knew only that his parents had been divorced and that neither of them had provided him with a home. Perhaps he needed my love even more than I needed his; perhaps he needed to love more than I needed it. I did not consciously deceive him about my feelings for him; perhaps, like me, he was content to settle for what he could have. My body was young and healthy and responded to his as much as he could have wished.

I had intended to book him a single room, in a hotel run by and for refugees, for the three days it took soldiers to get a marriage license. But the only room available was a double one, and so we decided that I should begin my stay there at once; there was a ten o'clock curfew for me. We thought that if we pretended to be already married it would save us a lot of embarrassment.

Would I prefer him not to share the double bed with me—just yet? Walter asked me. Of course I wanted us to share it; we had such a brief time together. Both of us were inexperienced and under-informed, and had gleaned from the literature of our adolescence that girls were likely to become pregnant the first time they had intercourse. His friends had equipped him with a stock of condoms, but had warned him that they were liable to tear while breaking a hymen. We were too embarrassed to discuss it. I had once seen a condom floating in the lavatory bowl at home without at the time knowing what it was. I had never seen an erect penis.

Though we shared the bed naked and spent much of the night awake, we stopped short of consummation. I was too ignorant to appreciate Walter's self-control. When we woke in the morning, he asked me, "Do you think that I might have done something to give you a baby?" I knew enough to be reassured by the absence of blood on the sheet.

I had taken time off from work but been asked to call in at the ORT office and, anxious to know what this was about, went there on Thursday morning while Walter went to see about the license. I was told that the ORT could not afford to continue to employ me; from now on the boys would have to do all their own housework. I was given two pounds in lieu of notice and the money in my hand was some consolation, so improvidently did I think at this time.

My memory's eye sees me on the flight of steps going up to the town hall: a small, slightly-built girl with a round and still childish face, and long hair of the darkest brown wavy about her shoulders. (She has been told that this makes her look German, but in spite of this—or to spite herself—she won't have it cut, rightly believing it to be the prettiest attribute of her appearance.) There is something about her large grey-green eyes, their heavy-lidded sadness perhaps, which brands her as Jewish. She looks about fifteen. With her is a young soldier, small for a man, with eyes like a puppy's and an apologetic smile, holding her summer-bare arm with his work-hardened hand. She doesn't understand where they are going, what she will have to do. "Leave everything to me," says the young man to whom she had entrusted herself, less from choice than out of necessity. She has very little faith in him, is tempted to pretend that they don't belong together, and does so in her mind. She is embarrassed, in front of the English town hall officials, by his foreignness, and believes that he is unaware both of the impression he makes and of her feelings about it.

They are told to sit down on a bench in the echoing corridor, among children and people who look like tramps. The girl doesn't see herself as one of the children because she doesn't see the soldier as an adult in charge of her; other people might. It doesn't show that she belongs with the tramps. The soldier whispers, too loudly, to reassure her; because of the sort of girl she is it has on her the opposite effect.

They are treated with special consideration, told to go in before those who have been waiting longer, presumably not because the official doesn't want foreigners hanging about his town hall but because the young man is wearing the king's uniform: he calls him "sir." But he is stopped just inside the door. The girl is encouraged to leave his side and come forward; in fact she is made to do so: she is the one of interest to this roomful of men in dark suits, fewer than they appear to be to her because she is afraid of them.

But, middle-class child as against all the odds she still is, demurely she does as she is told. "Stand here"—"Put your hand on this book and swear. . . ." It is the wrong Bible. There is too much of it: more than she is entitled to, including as it does the New Testament. Moreover, embossed on the cover is a cross, that symbol of barbarity, common in its day, which two thousand years later still signifies salvation through suffering as if that carpenter's son from Nazareth had been the only Jew who has ever been persecuted. . . . They exchanged it for a slim volume, which is all a Jew needs. But this show of delicacy makes this child feel deprived, discriminated against.

The questions, coming from an elderly, fatherly man sitting among his peers, are easy to answer. She doesn't know what she is being tested for but she will, as always, acquit herself with colours flying—or does one say flying colours?

"Are you still in communication with your parents?"

"Now that my sister is in the ATS—" Believing that maybe she is being tested for her attitude to the war, she is surprised at their indifference. Without emotion, because her parents have ceased to matter to her—she has succeeded in relegating them to the very margin of her world, from where they are about to be shrugged off into oblivion—she explains, "We exchange letters through the Red Cross." And wonders if this will count against her as "communicating with the enemy."

"You say that your parents know this young man?" She isn't aware of having told them this. "Is there a reason why you cannot write to them for permission and await their answer, before getting married?"

At last she understands what this is about, and hates the young man who is the cause of what to her is an ordeal, all the more so for being conducted in such a civilised manner. She is so naive that she doesn't understand that what she is being asked is, are you pregnant?

"No, no reason," she answers, thinking that given more warning she could have invented one. She still wants to get married, but now only because her insecurity makes her loathe changes of plan.

And then they're out of there and back in the sunshine on the town hall steps. "What am I going to say to my mates?" the young man asks, not of her but himself; he is red in the face with embarrassment as he remembers that they have clubbed together to buy him a wedding-present: a writing case of real leather which, seeing that she coveted it so, he has already handed over to his putative bride.

The girl—who stopped being anyone's child more than two and a half years ago—is thinking of what he did to her the night before in the double bed, and that she has lost her job, and that she has spent her savings on a white blouse to be married in which now she will not need.

That morning at breakfast in the dining-room, we had been teased because someone had noticed that I wasn't wearing a wedding-ring. No doubt word had got around that we were sharing a bed. Walter and I decided to keep the magistrates court's proceedings a secret, and as if we believed that the other people in the hotel really cared what we did—because we were all refugees—we agreed to brazen it out.

Did I want an engagement ring? Walter asked me. I said that I would rather have a watch. But first we went about Leeds from one post office to another: Red Cross letter forms were freely available, but they were useless without an international reply coupon, and these, where they were still available, were doled out one at a time. The letters, or the answers, did not always arrive. We persevered until we had three, and that evening wrote to my parents three identical letters of the permitted twenty-five words, including our signatures.

I had thought for some time that Irma and Ilse were better off than I was: they could eat as much as they wished without counting the cost, and had the freedom of a whole house which they frequently and for hours at a time had to themselves. Maids were becoming scarce; one was supposed to get one's job through the labour exchange, but the newspapers were full of advertisements and I was excited by the prospect of having a choice.

The job at the ORT had been offered to me: I had no experience of applying for a job. Though the reference they had given me was a good one, was better than I deserved, I had been there for only seven weeks, and this fact required so much explaining that I preferred not to show it. I had not got over my childhood fear of the telephone and hated needing to phone for appointments: the instrument made my English sound very much worse than it was. The nicer the house looked, the more I thought that I would like to live there, the harder I found it to go up to the door and ring the bell. I feared being confronted with strangers, feared needing to speak to them, did not know what to say, or not how to say it in English; my shyness magnified by embarrassment must have made me appear rather stupid. I did not know what wage to ask for: not wanting to give people cause to say that Jews were greedy but feeling justified in wanting every penny I could get. None of my earnings would have to be spent on necessities: this was what made me persevere in going to house after house—as did the impossibility of continuing without working.

The Duchamps had a two-year-old daughter and when I called at their house, only she and her nanny were at home. Amy was also a refugee, was a former schoolteacher from Vienna, in her late twenties. The relief I felt to be talking to her, to be shown round the house by her, misled me into seeing her as a friend, and the household as one which would suit me. The Duchamps were also Jewish. He was a general practitioner. She did all the cooking; all I would need to do was keep the house clean, Amy told me. After the hostels it did not even seem large. She showed me what would be my room and my mind was made up: I had not had such a nice bedroom even in my last years at home.

The cleaning I was expected to do took all morning; one afternoon I spent washing, one I spent ironing, one cleaning windows, one "turning out" one of the rooms, in rotation, one doing odd jobs such as cleaning the oven and polishing the silver. It was not the work I found irksome but my position. Apart from my one afternoon and one evening a week off I was expected not to leave the house; I was always at everyone's—even Amy's—beck and call. I needed to knock on doors, but Mrs. Duchamps went freely into my room—she once told me off for leaving my fountain-pen lying on the bedspread. Dr. Duchamps told me off for using the front door. Amy and I ate in the kitchen; even on the High Holy Days, when I waited at table also on the two Jewish soldiers—no less strangers to the Duchamps than we—who were there as their guests. When Mrs. Duchamps discovered that I wanted to leave, she said to Amy, "I took her in off the street and gave her a home; she's being ungrateful." And from the newspapers which were given to me to light the fires, she first removed the pages on which jobs were advertised.

Irma and Ilse had decided to join the ATS. Always easily influenced, I thought it a good idea: Anne had said that, wearing uniform and speaking with a foreign accent, you could not be assessed socially and so everybody treated you as an equal. I went with them to put my name down at the recruiting office. But then I changed my mind, partly because I was told that I would not necessarily be posted to my sister's unit, and partly because I thought that Anne might not like it if I were also to join up: when we were children she had not liked it when first Lise and then I followed her from school to school. One did not join Anne at anything without her permission and I lacked the courage to ask her for it, for fear of refusal. But chiefly I could not face committing myself for an indefinite time to a way of life. I could not even first try it out. The thought of helping to win the war against Hitler did not come into it: I saw myself as too insignificant to be able to do that.

Mrs. Duchamps found out that I wanted to leave her because the first job I applied for was offered to me by one of her friends. He was the manager of a garment factory. "You can do better than be a machinist," he told me, and promised to take me into his office once my English improved—which I knew it would do as soon as I would feel more at ease with him. While I was on my way back he phoned Mrs. Duchamps. Amy overheard her accusing me of all sorts of things: because she didn't want to lose me.

I was being paid fifteen shillings a week and had saved most of it. I decided that, first of all, I must find somewhere else to stay. On my evenings off I went to the cinema; I could not think of anything else to do in the blackout and I liked being among people without needing to speak with them. I had always told myself stories and was addicted to fiction. And I could not have faced finding my way about unlit residential streets. But on my afternoon off I found a room, easily: in a house given over altogether to lodgers; the landlord lived next door. He told me, "You can come and go as you please, no one will bother about you."

That evening, I sat in the Duchamps' kitchen and cried and could not stop crying. "Silly girl, it's your choice," Mrs. Duchamps pointed out. I could not explain to her, because I barely understood it myself, that I was not crying about leaving her but about having nowhere, nowhere where I wanted to be.

I had paid a week's rent in advance, but I did not go back to that house where no one would bother about me.

I was fortunate to find, instead, an attic to rent from a Jewish couple whose parents had immigrated from eastern Europe, and who therefore had some understanding of my circumstances. They had two delightful small girls and the happy family life shone into my solitude as if it were sunshine.

After I had moved in I went to the labour exchange, to the adult section, as I had meanwhile turned eighteen. The girl behind the counter could not have been much older than I. But with make-up on her face, with her hair professionally set and her nails manicured and, above all, her air of owning the space she occupied, she seemed adult to me and the contrast between us made me feel that I was not an applicant but a beggar.

What work had I been doing? she asked, and from her card-index began to read out details of domestic job vacancies. I feared to displease her by interrupting; I feared more to displease her by allowing her to go on when this was not what I was looking for. Aware that I was not sounding as if I deserved it, I told her that I was hoping for something better.

She flicked the card-index with her long red nails and then gave me a look which made me lower my eyes. "There's nothing else here for you," she said. "All the other jobs are of national importance, to help the war effort."

I had needed somebody to tell me that even I might be capable of doing that. "Oh, I would like to help the war effort," I said fervently.

"But you're a German!" she exclaimed, loud enough for everyone who was in that place to hear her. There was a hush after they all stopped speaking, during which they looked at me. "You must want Hitler to win the war," she added.

Under a lesser slander I might have cringed. But this was a challenge to which, little and lost as I was, I could only rise. I told her, "I have more reason to hate Hitler than you have!" my heart quaking as I thought of the reasons I had for hating him.

"You can say that," she said. "But I don't have to believe you."

I remained standing there for a moment longer, wondering if it were worth what it would cost me to try to make her understand my position, reconciling myself to my inadequacies: to do it I would have needed to be an English Gentile—but then I would not have had these devastating emotions so incomprehensibly alien to people like her.

When I applied for a job in Lewis's department store, I was asked if I wanted to work on the floor or in the counting house. I did not know what either expression meant but was too ashamed of my ignorance to say so. What was the difference? I asked the woman who was interviewing me. She explained that the starting wage was better on the floor, and that to get into the counting house I would need to pass an examination. She seemed to expect me to choose this and I couldn't understand why.

I became a junior in the dress department. Unpacking and ironing dresses, running errands for my superiors, was pleasant enough; I liked being one of a team. I liked especially the feeling of privilege it gave me to enter by an almost secret door before the store was opened to the public, to move about freely behind the scenes where customers weren't allowed, and to be there without wearing a coat as if I were at home.

I had been told that my weekly wage was twenty-five shillings. When I got my first pay-packet—on a Thursday evening to encourage us to do our shopping on Fridays rather than Saturdays: we got a staff discount—it contained only eighteen shillings and a few pence. Convinced that a mistake had been made, I rushed upstairs to the personnel manager, who explained to me that money had been deducted for my lunches and teas—which I had believed to be free—and for insurance stamps. "But this isn't enough to live on!" I exclaimed, already in tears before the man explained, kindly, that I was being paid according to my age and that girls of my age were expected still to be living at home.

Not wanting to embarrass him, who gave me the impression that he would have helped me if he could, I left and returned to my department, deciding on the way that I needed to find another job, better-paid. But I could not face once more starting all over again: finding my way to a new place, addressing strangers, explaining my circumstances, exposing myself to being questioned, to being doubted, being asked, "How much do you think you are worth?" and to the after-pains of having been rejected without quite understanding why. This was my third job in little more than four months, and each time I had been confident with hope—what reason had I for believing that among the choices I had there was one I could live with? I felt responsible for my circumstances, felt that they would not be as they were if I hadn't deserved them. This was what caused my tears to flow as if to drown the world.

I sat in the cubicle where I did the ironing and wept like a child for mankind to take pity on me. Several of the assistants were Jewish and all of them were friendly. They put their heads together and one of them came to tell me that they were collecting money for me to buy a black dress: they believed that I had been summoned by the personnel manager to be told off for not yet wearing one. It made me howl with anguish, to realise how simple to solve they believed my problem to be.

I remained working in Lewis's until the pantomime season, and until then I remained living with the Flowers—my seventh address in the less than three years I had been in England. They reduced my rent from ten shillings to nine to help me make ends meet. Whenever I was there at mealtimes they fed me, especially on Sundays. I shared their living-room and felt as at home with them as I was capable of doing with strangers. Mrs. Flowers encouraged me to borrow her clothes, especially her warm winter coat since I had none; she took an interest in my appearance, persuading me to wear lipstick and a roll-on. I tried to make myself over to be as she and the assistants in Lewis's saw me.

Walter came on leave. He slept in my bed in the attic while I slept next to the seven-year-old Judith in Diana's bed, who was moved back into her cot. After everyone was asleep, Walter visited me and with kisses and cuddles prompted me to follow him up the stairs. Our fear of making a baby preserved my virginity.

The most important event for me in those ten or eleven weeks was an entertainment put on by the Free German Youth, to which I contributed a longish poem for several voices and chorus. I have forgotten every word of it, most probably it made the point that Germany must not be equated with Hitler; I may have called him a carbuncle on the face of German history. I had rehearsed the speakers, but now I sat in the audience, and afterwards overheard people praising the piece while ignoring me as someone of no importance: a situation from which I derived a satisfaction the greater for it being secret and mine alone.

But I did not want to identify with these exiles who continued to think of themselves as Germans. My father thought of himself as a German whose religion happened to be Jewish, and as he was irreligious this made him—in his own eyes—much more of a German than a Jew. But the times I had been born into had conditioned me to see myself as a Jew who happened to have been born in Germany.

After that evening, I had nothing more to do with the FDJ, and ceased to value the poems I wrote in German.

December 1941–February 1942

(Bury to Bradford)

To call it my first dance, I wrote to Walter, might be misleading because that was how one would also refer to an opening waltz; perhaps the proper term for it was "my first ball." But the Lewis's first floor staff party was light-years away from the world of Jane Austen which I was thinking of. It took place in a shabby hall above a public house, and was also the first occasion on which I drank something stronger than sacramental wine.

A moralist might have seen it as auguring worse to come.

As I had nothing suitable to wear, and could not afford to buy even one of our cheapest dresses even with a staff discount, I had bought a length of plum-coloured satin of the sort that was meant to be used as lining, and designed a dress with a tight bodice and a flared skirt, which I stitched on the sewing machine of one of Mrs. Flowers's friends. We changed, after work, in the department; the others, with a communal effort, made up my face. I felt like a whore and maybe I looked like one.

Seeing what competition there was, I did not dare to compete for the attention of the personnel manager: he was the most eligible young man there. He sought me out, and I wondered if he did so because he recognised me as the girl who had wept in his office. Since I didn't know how to dance he held me very tightly, almost lifting me off my feet; it did not seem to me that what he was feeling for me could be compassion. I remembered what Annie, the Irish cook for Irma's household, had said: certainly I preferred this man to Walter; but I knew him to be altogether beyond my reach.

This was the one time in my life when, for a few weeks, I ceased to feel inferior about my looks. I was about to become a chorus girl. On the day of the staff party I had already given my notice.

Naively, I took the job because it offered more money. When Mrs. Flowers told me that, if I valued my relationship with Walter, I ought to write and ask him for his permission, I could not understand why she should think this necessary. He was sending me money, but beyond that he was not helping me to live. I thought too little of him (if he could love me he couldn't amount to much) to be willing to see myself as emotionally dependent on him; wrongly I believed that I wasn't. I wrote to Anne, asking her opinion, instead, and as always she answered me that as far as my life was concerned I had to decide for myself.

I had not been seriously looking for another job; the advertisement caught my eye because it was a display one. It said, "Girls wanted for pantomime chorus. No experience necessary. £1 weekly all found." It was the "all found" which hooked me: I did not know what to make of the expression, but it sounded to me like a promise that I would be looked after. Seven months after I had run away to independence, this was for me the flesh-pots which I yearned for.

The address, to which I went that very evening, turned out to be one in a row of semi-detached bungalows. In the blackout, my torch could not find the number, but I knew the house by the sounds of entertainment coming from it. The front door was ajar in spite of the blackout and the freezing night. The sitting-room which I found my way into was over-heated and crowded with mothers and small girls.

Pearl was fat and jovial, no longer young enough to work as a dancer but not old. "Show us your legs," she told me, cutting short my stammered enquiry. I raised my skirt above my knees. "Higher." I complied. "You'll do," she said, and I knew that I had been wrong: it wasn't my hair—my legs were what was best about my appearance.

From when I was a child, I have not liked to ask questions: betraying my ignorance. I did not know that the pantomime I was to be in was *Robinson Crusoe* until I saw a poster for it at the railway station in Bury. We were to rehearse there for a week, before opening there, and then going on tour, to Stockport and four other towns around Manchester, appearing in each for a week.

Before I could accept the job, I needed police permission to be out in the streets after ten o'clock. I went to the headquarters in Leeds and there they endorsed my Aliens Registration book accordingly. When I asked what I should do about my temporary changes of address, they offered to phone their colleagues on my behalf. They were at ease with me, joked with me, made me feel that since my visit to the police station in Ruthin I had made a good deal of progress and not only in my knowledge of English. Whatever reservations Mrs. Flowers had about my becoming a chorus girl, policemen evidently liked me the better for it.

I would not have minded being Jean or Peggy or any one of the six professional dancers of the senior chorus; they knew how to make the most of their looks and were quick at repartee with the men and, above all, had self-confidence. For a time, there was nothing I wanted more than I wanted to be allowed to belong with them. I danced with them—if my copying of their movements could be called dancing; I mouthed the words they sang, afraid to let my voice be heard because I could not carry a tune. When I had confessed this to Pearl she had said that my legs made up for it. She was providing two seniors. Mary was only fourteen, though big for her age; she was rather simple-minded. She didn't count with me and neither of us counted with the six others.

Outside the theatre, she and I, as Pearl's girls, belonged with the eight members of the junior chorus. It included three sisters, whose mother had been engaged to look after us all. I observed Mrs. Judd being a mother to her daughters and coveted her for myself. I had practised on Walter wanting what I could have since I couldn't have what I wanted; I was becoming good at it. I had suffered too much from being seen as inferior to look down upon anyone. Since becoming an English Gentile was better than being a German Jew—who was I to question the judgment of the majority?—Mrs. Judd and her daughters—and everybody around me—must, I thought, be better than I was, and what I aspired to was being accepted by them as one of themselves.

There was nothing I could do about being who I was. But since I didn't want to be who I was, didn't value it, I was ready to put on camouflage; to do so was a relief to me. Experience had taught me that to admit that I was a Jew did not instantly make people understand my refugee status: henceforth I would keep hidden what was such a burden to me. I could not have brought myself to say that I was a German even if, in wartime England, this had not been an even worse disadvantage. I had had a French step-grandmother. With a lack of inventiveness which still shames my imagination, I told the pantomime people that I was French. To explain my German accent—and my lack of French—I said that my family had been living in Germany. They had been itinerant show-people, I said, making my bid to belong, resurrecting my childhood fantasy of running away with the gipsies. To invent such parents for myself helped me to see myself as I wanted others to see me. Nobody was sufficiently interested in my background to give me the chance to elaborate on it, which I would have enjoyed doing. That maybe they didn't believe me occurs to me only now.

When I was five or six years old, a girl in our street appeared as one of Snow White's seven dwarfs in a pantomime put on in our municipal theatre; all the neighbourhood children were given complimentary tickets. Apart from this I had not been in a theatre either in Germany or England, until Bury. I had no standard by which to judge our company; I ought to have known that it must be third-rate to have engaged someone like me. But so much in those days was makeshift because of the war, and probably I needed to have illusions. I knew from books that things looked different from our side of the footlights.

It did nothing for me to be accepted as a dancer, in the sense in which being accepted as a poet would have done something for me; but it has always been part of my nature to want to excel, to make up with tenacity for what I lack in talent.

"That Frenchy," the men standing watching in the wings commented, and I felt reassured because when we came off there was always someone who detained me with small talk. I once missed a whole routine because the manager of the theatre was talking to me and I believed that politeness demanded that I should continue to stand there and listen. "All right for some," one of my peers said to the others, passing me as they came off; it was something to be remembered against me. I fraternized with the stage-hands when they took notice of me, before somebody told me that this was not done.

In time I became friendly with the Judd sisters, especially with Alice, the eldest, who was not much younger than I but so undersized as to be still dancing in the junior chorus. She had been dancing in pantomimes almost since she could walk, and had her own dancing-school in the front room of her home.

She told me that I offended people by refusing the cigarettes they offered. "I don't smoke," I pointed out, and she said, "That's what I mean." Wanting to be accepted above all socially, I started to smoke. I didn't know that I mustn't accept whole packs until she told me. She reminded me that, at the first rehearsal, I had gone up to the piano as if I were "more important than anyone else." I explained that I had thought that I might be able to read the music. "Well it gave us all the impression that you're terribly stuck up."

There were three comedians in the company; I have forgotten which one was considered the first. One was a small, bullet-headed man, who tried to allocate a speaking part to me. "What's your name?" he asked, to which I had to answer, "Basil."—"Basil what?"—"Basil'll do if they haven't a Guinness." I had come across the name Basil in Keats. But I didn't know that the other names were those of drinks, nor that the line was meant to be funny. He dropped the idea when the other girls objected to his spending so much rehearsal time on me.

They also resented the attention I was getting from the other comedians, both called Joe and both, I think, in their forties. One, who played the Dame, was tall and lanky; his special act was a tap-dance in wooden shoes with very long toes.

The other was short and balding, and was billed as "the only human billiard-table": for this act he dressed in bright green, with pockets in various places into which he rolled the balls across his back.

I overheard somebody saying, "If Joe likes a girl he will do anything for her." Since my life was suffering from a shortage of people who would do something, let alone anything for me—only Walter would—I thought it important to find out which of them had been meant.

While we were still in rehearsal, first one and then the other asked me out for the evening. Since both were inviting me to go to a pub, and I didn't know which one of them ought not to be offended, I suggested that we should all three go together. Actually, other members of the company came as well and for a while we all sat as a group.

I had never been in a bar before, and when offered a drink did not know what to ask for. Gin and lime, I think it was, tall Joe suggested I should have, "A drink for a lady." No one had ever before implied that I was a lady; and I liked the taste. The next morning, short Joe told me that when he saw that the other Joe intended to get me drunk, he left us to it.

The group melted away: either because the others left or because I could no longer see them, or anything, clearly. Tall Joe helped me out into the night. The air was frosty and the stars were sparkling. He put his arm firmly about me—through my raincoat, my jumper, my vest and bra I could feel his hand on my breast and I liked the feeling. We had the blacked-out street to ourselves; perhaps it was already very late or, more likely, he steered me to where there was no one about. He stood me against a wall and kept me there by pressing against me.

He kissed me; he put his hand inside my clothing. By my reaction he must have known it, he asked, "Are you still a virgin?" I told him that I was. "Oh, baby," he said.

I remember standing there, looking past the man's head at the stars; I knew the English names of some of the constellations, had memorised them for use in my poetry. "Oh, baby," he said again. No one had ever called me that and it sounded sweet to me. His face against mine, I could feel the breath of his voice; our physical closeness made him seem to be my friend. If such friendship between strangers could be achieved, so quickly, easily, lightly, through touching, I thought, then to let his hand do as it wished was a small price for me to pay.

The next morning, at rehearsal, he greeted me with, "I kept my head, didn't I," and a wink which made me believe that what had happened between us was the beginning of a relationship. Sober, and by morning light, I found him less appealing; his eyes were watery, his cheeks veined, his teeth bad: a man who had once been handsome running to seed. It would not have mattered if he had been willing to continue to show me the affection which I needed so much from someone, anyone. But he must have concluded that to buy me drinks was a waste of money, to spend an evening with me a waste of time.

The comment I had overheard must have referred to billiard-table Joe; it wasn't true of him either, but he was a kinder man. I have no idea if the other Joe told him what had or rather what had not happened. He apologised for having deserted me, with the peace-offering of a packet of cigarettes. I have forgotten what they were called; they came in a red box with a cat embossed on it: which was what had made me choose this particular brand. I found it touching that Joe should have known that this was the one I smoked.

He had been in show-business all his life, had a unique act—

or so he said and I believed him; the writer in me was interested in what he could tell me. He was not easy to talk with, being slightly deaf, and pretending not to be able to hear any question he preferred not to answer, questions about his personal life for instance.

In the course of the tour, I went several times to his lodgings, between a matinee and an evening show; he gave me tea and did not try to touch me. I persisted partly because I needed a friend and even he was better than no one, and partly because I was curious to find out why he was befriending me. Perhaps he just liked to be seen escorting me.

During our week of rehearsal, there was a variety show on in the theatre to which we were admitted free and went repeatedly; there wasn't much else to do in the evenings and it was better than sitting in our lodgings. One of the acts was acrobatics by a troupe of Moroccans, billed as Ali and his family. It included an older man and several children. That Ali lodged by himself probably means that he was not a relation at all. But he was the star.

He was a small man, compactly built like a boxer, thirty years old at most, with a handsome face, and attractive across the footlights. The sight of him reminded me of a gipsy boy I had fleetingly known in the happiest summer of my childhood—or what in retrospect seems to have been the happiest: the one before Hitler came to power, the one of my ninth birthday. According to the posters, Ali and his family had before the war toured the world with a famous circus; no doubt this was meant to impress and it impressed me.

When I told Joe that I would like to talk with Ali, he took me backstage and introduced me to him. I don't remember—I don't know if I ever knew whether these two men were already known to each other. Joe arranged with Ali to bring me, the next afternoon, to his lodging.

It ought to have warned me when he left me at the street door. He said that there was something else he needed to do and, though I told lies myself, I always naively believed what others told me. The door was opened by Ali himself; it led up a bleak staircase straight into an attic room. Before discarding my raincoat, I took my notebook and pencil from its pockets; I had still not adopted an adult woman's practice of using a handbag. I thought that I had made it clear to Joe that I wanted to interview the man; either Joe had not heard, or not understood, or not believed it, or not passed the information on. The only chair in the room had Ali's jacket draped over the back; I therefore thought nothing of it when he indicated that I should sit down on the bed.

The next moment, I found myself lying on it, with him on top of me, his trousers about his ankles. More than anything else I felt surprise: because I had not even noticed him undoing them. I struggled; when he understood that my refusal was meant, he got off me and allowed me to get up. I did not look at him, I was so ashamed of having been thought of as he had thought of me. My notebook and pencil I left behind in my haste to escape.

My innocence would not be credible if it had not been true: even after this I fell in with Joe's suggestion, a week or two later, to visit Ali in Manchester, where he and his troupe were appearing in a circus. I welcomed the break in the routine, believed that it would make an interesting outing.

Ali must have been expecting us: his landlady provided, with a pot of tea, a plateful of home-made iced queen cakes, a real treat in those days of rationing. But when Joe excused himself, I quickly got up as well; I remember that what I feared was less being left alone with Ali than being alone in Manchester and not knowing how to get back to Stockport.

Knowing that I was used to looking after myself, Mrs. Judd treated me as an equal. Maybe this was what prompted Alice to accept me as a friend, and made her sisters look up to me. Most of my time was spent in their company. We went about together with Pearl's other girls, to the cinema for instance; we were all issued with free passes. We ate together and slept together, usually sharing rooms and for at least one week four of us sharing one double bed. I had not been able to blend in—in Dovercourt, in Whittingehame, in Nanclwyd Lodge—with people with whom I had much in common. Like a child who believes himself to be invisible with closed eyes, I still believed that because I wanted to belong, because I felt the need to belong, I would be able to do so.

"It's the way you look," Alice answered when I asked her if she knew why the other girls didn't like me. "With your hair so plain and no make-up."—"I use lipstick," I pointed out. I also used a touch of it on my cheeks, never without remembering how much it had worried my mother that I was always so pale. "You should use make-up on your eyes," Alice advised me, "to stop them from looking so sad."

And what was wrong with my hair? If I made it curl more it would soften my whole appearance. One rainy afternoon without a matinee, she put it for me into metal rollers, after heating them in the oven. When she took them out of my hair, it hung in ringlets all over, and when she had finished applying make-up and allowed me to look in a mirror, I liked the result: so unlike myself did I look.

I was not aware of it at the time, but becoming a chorus girl was also a running away, meant breaking with my past at a profounder level than when I had left *hachsharah.* The total break with my parents happened at about this time; I received what was to be their last letter to me in January 1942. I was still too much of a child—had believed in the existence of God for too long—to have accommodated my feelings to the idea that the forces governing my life were neutral. It was in rebellion against what had happened to me—so long as I didn't submit to it passively I need not see myself as a victim—that I helped it along now by letting go of that lifeline to my past: my relationship with Walter. I stopped writing to him and he did not know where I was.

I had heard often enough that all that counted with Jews was money, to accept as my reason for not wanting to return to

Leeds my conscious thought that there my wages had not been enough to live on. If I came to Bradford, Alice told me, I would be able to find better-paid work in a mill, and her mother said that I would be able to stay with them.

I listened to them talking about their going home at the end of the tour, about my coming home with them, and in my destitution and need clutched at the belief that, they being my friends, the place they were talking about would become home to me, too.

Once again, nothing turned out to be at all as I had imagined it.

"I'll be glad to get home," Mrs. Judd sighed repeatedly during the last days of the tour, causing me to expect something better than our lodgings, which were rated good only because there was no vermin. "We've a modern house," she told me; but all she meant was that it had an indoor lavatory. To my eyes it wasn't a real house at all, being merely a section of a long low terrace, with small, over-furnished, unaired, lightless rooms, and not many of them. Where am I going to sleep? I wondered as the girls showed me round, and for the rest of the evening, before I found out: on the couch in the living-room, with a cushion instead of a pillow, and Mr. Judd's winter coat—smelling of pipe tobacco—to supplement the blankets.

"You'll like our Dad," Mrs. Judd and her daughters had said. "He's a caution." But they had omitted to warn him that they were bringing me; perhaps he resented not having been asked beforehand for his permission, He had been expecting them back: had got the tea ready but, of course, had not set a place or bought a meat pie for me. Never since coming to England had I been made to feel so unwelcome.

At the beginning of the tour, I had opened a post office savings account; of the seven pounds I had earned, I had paid into it five pounds and ten shillings. Mrs. Judd knew how much money I had: I had boasted to her of it. It did not occur to me that she might be expecting to be paid for having me stay: nothing had been said about that when she had invited me, and

I believed that she understood my emotional need to hold on to these savings, which were my safety net.

I was not looking for a holiday; it would have suited me to start working in a mill the following morning. I am not sure now why I didn't do so: because I discovered that Alice and her family thought her above such work (Annie and Mildred went back to school); or because I was told that it counted as war work, which meant that once I had taken such a job, I would be committed to it for the duration? I remember walking about the centre of Bradford, bracing myself to go into one shop after another and telling the owner or the manager that my parents had had a shop just like it, somewhere in France. . . .

After Mr. Judd had made it clear to his wife, and she to me, that I could not continue to stay with them, there were days when I walked about the residential streets, calling at houses with ROOM TO LET signs in their windows. One woman, after questioning me, turned me away for being a foreigner. Another, a few doors along in the same street, said, "You look too young to be living away from your parents," and even if I could have mustered self-control enough to explain my circumstances, it would not have helped me, because she had already shut me out.

It cannot be true, that while I was working as a mill girl I never saw daylight, but that is how I remember it. I slept in the attic with Irene, who was my age: sharing her single-sized bed. We got up before dawn, still partly dressed from the day before against the cold. Because of the skylight above, which was not blacked-out, the stairs were unlit; on my first morning there, unfamiliar with the lay-out, I walked into the banister and broke it; I still bear the scar on my knee-cap. Mrs. Graham would already be up, with a napkin airing in front of the fire and the son she had borne in her middle-age on his potty beside the table on which she had set out our breakfast. The tea reminded me of Dovercourt, and tasted worse because now sugar was rationed.

There was a bathroom; but on weekdays we had only a token, cold-water wash at the kitchen sink. Irene had her hair done professionally once a month; she slept with a net over it; I never saw her comb it. Mindful of what Alice had told me, I put mine overnight into curlers, and out of doors protected it with a headscarf, like most girls and women I came into contact with.

By starlight we ran to the bus stop, chasing clouds of our breath; kept waiting there, we clapped our hands and stamped our feet against the winter cold.

It was dark again by the time we finished work.

But now I remember that we left the mill at noon, and walked the short distance to the home of Irene's aunt, who gave us lunch; mine was paid for out of the eighteen shillings which I gave Irene's mum for my bed and board. I earned thirty-two shillings a week and received about thirty.

Both my job and my lodgings had been arranged for me by the Judds; the Grahams were their relations. Before I moved from the one house to the other, I made a day-trip to Leeds, to collect what belongings I had left with the Flowers, though I had, naturally, given up my room there. Mrs. Flowers told me that Walter had in the meantime visited them, hoping that they would be able to tell him my address. He had given her some money to keep my room for me in case I decided that I still wanted it.

I could not have explained then—did not understand—that I could not remain there because I was trying to run away from myself.

Some letters had come for me: one from Anne, and two identical Red Cross forms from my parents giving me their permission to marry Walter and adding that they were about to go on a journey. I believed that the reason why this was all they said about it was that they were allowed to write no more than twenty-five words.

After Anne and Lise and I had left them, our parents had moved from the flat in which we had all last lived together. I knew the street in which they had been living since, it was close to the synagogue—close to where the synagogue had been. While Anne had still been interned on the Isle of Man, through her, I had received photographs which my father had taken of their one room and a half in a "Jews' House": the partition between them and another couple was only a blanket. On the backs, my mother had in her small neat script written precise descriptions. I had not looked at the pictures, nor read the words; I could not bear to think of them as having adjusted to living without me. I had convinced myself that I was no longer interested in them, whose lives no longer had anything to do with mine.

The machines, rows upon rows of them in a large hall reverberating with their noise, spun thread for army blankets, transferring it from one bobbin to another, refining it on the way by means of the tension and of sharp-edged loops. There were many bobbins in each row, many rows on each machine; my job was to keep them turning by knotting the thread when it broke, which was often, and by replacing the bobbins at one end of the process when they were empty, and at the other end when they were full. It meant being on one's feet and surrounded by machine noise for eight hours each day, but I did not mind the work. To amuse myself, I tried to beat the machine by having all the bobbins spinning at once; it could not be done often or for long. Another pastime was to go to the lavatory for a smoke; if one did this too often or stayed for too long, the foreman would come right in there and fetch one out.

The machines stood back to back; because of the noise it was not easy to communicate with one's partner. Mine was a tall young woman, platinum blonde, with full lips and full breasts, of which I was envious. She sang all day long, at the top of her voice, the popular wartime songs, or else she shouted across to me, in detail, the story of the film she had just seen; she seemed to spend every evening at the cinema. Because of the curfew in force for aliens, I could go only on Saturday afternoons: there was not time, between my finishing work and my needing to be indoors, to see the full programme, which in those days ran continuously—even if I had been willing to see the end of a film before seeing the beginning, and to forgo my evening meal.

Of course I knew that this was not the only difference between us; but I used to think that if I were able to go to the cinema as often as she I would be as happy.

Reunion

It is the first occasion I can remember on which I am carrying a handbag. It is large enough to take a Penguin book as well as my lipstick, handkerchief, etc., is shaped like an envelope, and consists of a thin layer of dark brown rilled leather over beige canvas-like material from which it will soon begin to flake off. Now it is still new, bought in Bradford and exactly like the one owned by the prettiest girl who danced in the senior chorus. Like people influenced by advertisements, I have bought it in the belief that its possession will help me to resemble her.

I remember it so exactly because of what was, on this occasion, among its contents: one of the copies of my parents' latest—the last, but I did not know that then—Red Cross letter giving me permission to marry the soldier in whose company I am. As if I were encased in armour I am cut off from him by the conflict raging within me. I cannot hear, I do not want to hear what he is telling me: the details of his Odyssey which has brought him to me. Instead of rejoicing in his resourcefulness, in this proof of his love for me, I wish with all my delinquent heart that he had failed in his quest and left me unconfronted with this need to make a decision.

How can I marry this man who has failed to understand that I did not want to be found by him or, having understood, has ignored what I wanted?

On the other hand, why should I go back on the decision which seemed right six months ago and of which my parents approve?

We are sitting opposite each other at a small round table, in a small cafe, of the sort in which, in those days, the waitresses wore housemaids' uniforms. They are waiting for us to leave; we are the last customers; it is almost closing time for them.

At home with my parents and sisters, my greed, especially for sweet foods, had been a joke; but now I have not finished my piece of cake, which looks better than it tastes: like everything else which life offers me nowadays, it is something I thought I wanted only until I have got it.

Walter is saying, "Let me look after you. Look what happens when you try to look after yourself!" I do not dare to ask him what he means, can instantly think of a number of things which have happened to me recently which I don't want him, or anybody, to know about. Feeling guilty makes me blush and he flashes his eyes at me. What is it he thinks I am thinking of?

He asks me something; I cannot, do not want to hear his question, instantly forget how it was worded, know only that it has entrapped me: it concerns my parents' letter. I cannot remember now and I could not remember then what it is doing inside my handbag, how it comes to be there, what thought or impulse prompted me to put it in there so that I have it with me now and in its presence cannot lie about it. I don't believe in God and I'm not superstitious, but I cannot tell a lie concerning my parents, not even about this letter the contents of which concern me more than it does them; never before in my life have I been constrained by a taboo against lying whenever it suited me. A few words would suffice to gain me three months' grace.

Don't I want it?

The moment for casual, believable lying has passed: nobody waiting for so long before giving an answer can do other than tell the truth. (Why would I have needed to think about what to say if I had not yet heard from them?) I bring my handbag up from my lap, open it, finger its scant contents, take out the letter—a small, smooth, flimsy piece of paper folded top and bottom against the middle; like that I pass it across the table littered with tea things to Walter, who could not ever have had any doubt about my parents' response. He is an unassuming young man—too unassuming for my taste—but he must have known, on the one hand how well my parents, how well everybody in the Bielefeld Jewish community had thought of him, and on the other, that my parents, who can no longer do anything for me, were bound, no matter with what misgivings, to do as I had asked.

He reads the letter, which does not take him long, and with his apologetic smile, which is one of the several things I don't really like, I really dislike about him, he asks, "Well then, shall we go ahead?" But it isn't a question: it feels to me as if he and my parents had arranged our marriage between them without consulting me, who does not want to get married, not to Walter or to anyone. Not because I don't want to have sex—I do, though perhaps, I think, rather with someone else whom I have not yet met—but because I want to remain autonomous.

The waitresses, standing about out of earshot but watching us, are aware that something has been decided; one of them comes to the table and hands Walter the bill. Though she calls him "sir," I think it is typical of him that he needs to be told to pay not her but at the cash-desk, and am embarrassed on his behalf. The thought occurs to me that I am about to entrust the management of my life to someone with no more talent for living than I have myself.

I would not call it a wedding, this attendance by Walter and me at the registry office to get the certificate which will entitle me to draw a soldier's wife's allowance and free me from all the restrictions applying to enemy aliens. In fact I can now stop lying about my nationality: henceforth I am Austrian because Walter was born in Salzburg. Irene's auntie thinks that Austrian is short for Australian and I marvel at the insularity of the British, who seem to forget that Hitler himself is an Austrian, and don't know that the Austrians are worse anti-Semites, and see them as the first victims of the Nazis.

To my mind, a wedding requires a bride in a white dress, with a veil, carrying flowers, attended by her family and friends; I have never been to a wedding and am unaware that what I am picturing is a scene from a film: a Christian ceremony. I would not bestow the term "ceremony" on what is taking place either; it is very unceremonious, and soon over.

Walter and I walk out of the building holding hands, as we came in holding hands; the only difference I am aware of is that the wedding-ring, which before was in one of Walter's pockets, is now on my finger. I am always so anxious about events that I want them (if they are what I want) to have happened rather than be happening: I am happier now that I am a married woman than I was a few moments ago while I was becoming one.

Walter says, "Now you'll have me, and you'll never be alone again."

It is not what I wanted to hear him say; I want him not to have said this; it is not even true: I feel more alone now than I normally do; I have been feeling more alone all morning, because joining my life to Walter's is something I have to do by myself. What I mean is that the event has made me realise how singular and alone every human being is and must be forever.

It has nothing to do with the absence of my mother and my father, of Anne and Lise; if even one of them could have been there—if I could have been together longer than fleetingly with any one of them I would not have had to get married, or at least not yet, and perhaps not to Walter. He is my Bielefeld. It doesn't seem fair to him, that I married him because of this instead of for himself. But he has got what he wanted; our marriage is also the result of his pursuit of me.

Like other young couples—it is only our circumstances which are different—we have got married also for the sake of having sex. He wants to have sex with me and to me having sex is synonymous with being married. I am young and healthy and normal and have discovered that the body is less complicated than the mind, at least I believe that this is what I have discovered: that it is easier to relate through touching than through talking; even babies can do it. Perhaps the explanation for what I feel about Walter is that we are better suited physically than mentally; this does not occur to me.

I accept as proof of my theory that I like being touched by him, seldom feel prompted to find fault with him over it, as I frequently do over hearing what he has to say. For instance, at breakfast that morning—we met in a cinema cafe before going to the registry office—he said, "If you want to change your mind it's not yet too late." I did but it was; if I could have mustered self-possession enough to walk out on him at this stage, I would never have passed the point of agreeing to marry him.

He is five years older than I am and, what probably makes a greater difference, he is the only son of divorced parents, while I am the youngest of three and have always been babied by all my family. The way his body relates to mine makes me feel good, encourages me not to think too badly of my body. But in conversation he has a way of responding which makes me feel patronised. For instance, he jeered at my suggestion that we should invite Mrs. Judd and her daughters to the registry office; they wanted to come and I felt that I owed it to them because they had befriended me—within their limitations; I can see as well as he can what these are, especially now that I no longer need them. Was it really better to have as our witnesses a janitor and a cleaning-woman, who obliged us because we paid them for it? Walter thought so, and I cannot, emotionally, afford to question his judgment.

That I have doubts about him is only to be expected: I have doubts about everybody, and most of all about myself.

March 1942–Anne's Death

(Dumfries–Edinburgh)

Walter was then stationed in Scotland, about half an hour's bus ride from Dumfries. I remained in Bradford, awaiting the arrival of my first soldier's wife's allowance book: cashing the counterfoils which would by then be due would provide me with my train fare and the security of a little money in hand. Also, he needed first to find me somewhere to stay.

He wrote that he had found a room, only a few minutes' walk from the gates of his camp. It was in a farmhouse, really part of its living quarters but partitioned off with a curtain. There was no electricity, no bathroom, and no water-closet but only a shed with a seat over a hole in the ground. He was living under canvas, so as far as he was concerned—he would be able to get a sleeping-out pass—even such accommodation was an improvement. But would I think his intermittent company compensation enough for the loss of amenities?

I wasn't sure; it meant going back to the living conditions of Nanclwyd Lodge, and now among strangers. But what choice did I have? In fact, Walter rented the room without awaiting my answer; his unit had been stationed in the same place for some time and all the better accommodation had already been taken. He, at least, was convinced that I needed to be with him more than I needed a water-closet, and that being my husband gave him the right to make decisions on my behalf. We both saw our roles as husband and wife much as our parents' generation had done.

Apart from the character reference I had been given by the ORT school, I had for all my varied work experience no references: had never remained for sufficiently long in one job. I hoped that—no longer being an enemy alien, or entirely dependent on my earnings—I would now be able to find more congenial work. Walter had spoken of me to the owner of a Dumfries bookshop; the man had promised to employ me—according to Walter, who had perhaps misunderstood him. When nothing came of this, naturally I believed that I must have made a bad impression. With every job I applied for in vain I became less capable of impressing prospective employers. Speaking to Scotsmen played havoc with my English; I still looked like a schoolgirl; I could still not explain my circumstances without betraying how I felt about them.

I could not bear to remain in the farmhouse all day, I felt too ill at ease there on my own; it was only Walter's presence which made the place acceptable to me. I continued to take the bus into Dumfries every morning, with the workers; needing somewhere to shelter from the still wintry weather led to my discovery of the public library.

That was where from then on I went and spent my days, reading. I would take a likely book from the shelf and stand there, pretending to myself that I was only browsing, that I was keeping an eye on the time, that presently I would look at the advertisements in the local newspaper, and go on applying for jobs; I would pretend to myself that it wasn't noon, that I wasn't hungry, that the day wasn't passing, that I would stop reading when I had finished this book. . . . I read as a frightened child covers its head with a blanket.

Perhaps the chief reason why I was keeping only such tenuous contact with Anne during these years was that I had never anything to report which would have made her feel pleased to have such a younger sister. And now I needed daily to account to Walter; being ashamed to tell him that I had still found nothing was what made me continue to look for work.

And then one day, in a back street near the town centre, in the window of an ironmonger's shop, I saw a hand-written notice: WANTED, OFFICE JUNIOR. An office job was the work I had always wished for most; for as long as I can remember I have had a passion for pens and pencils and every kind of paper: the tools of my trade. The window was full of objects I had never knowingly seen before, nor knew the names of; it looked as if the display had not been changed in years. The shop was long and narrow and dark, and crammed with things. Beyond the long counter there stood—dividing the shop from the store-room at the back—a sort of wood-and-glass cage; out of it came a young woman with a round and smiling face. She looked as unlikely as I felt to be working in an ironmonger's.

It echoed my experience of getting the job as housemaid at the Duchamps': Nancy interviewed me and promised to make sure that I would be hired. She had been working for Mr. Jackson since leaving school and now wanted to get married, but had promised him not to leave until she had trained her successor.

Nancy and Mr. Jackson talked of going abroad when they meant, to Carlisle. Letters in that office were still written by hand, in a special ink so that an impression could be transferred into a manuscript book, as used to be done in solicitors' offices. Mr. Jackson offered me a starting wage of fifteen shillings, which was what Nancy had received on starting twelve years before; she got him to agree to pay me a guinea until he had satisfied himself that I deserved as much as she was getting, which was twenty-five shillings.

"If nothing's sold there's no need to keep books," Mr. Jackson was fond of saying, expecting me from the first also to serve in the shop, though customers needed to describe to me what they wanted because I didn't know what things were called, and then I didn't know where they were kept. Small items in infrequent demand were stored among the rafters; fetching them meant climbing up a ladder and balancing along beams. "Three-quarter inch tower bolts!" Mr. Jackson shouted at me. "Where have you been all your life that you don't know what tower bolts look like!" I dreaded needing to accept orders over the telephone: the combination of the farmers' accent and my ignorance of the trade. I had thought that "galvanized" described a state of mind, and how could anything be "pale" in inches? But as with dancing in the pantomime chorus, I saw the job as a challenge, and that I was able to do it helped to mend my pride.

By the autumn I was settled in Edinburgh, where I was to remain until after the end of the war.

To begin with, out of consideration for one of his fellow soldiers whose family needed the money, Walter rented for me a room in what I think must have been a council house, in one of the suburbs. No previous landlady, not even the non-Jewish ones, had ever made me feel as uncomfortable as this Orthodox Jewess. She disapproved of me: for not dressing modestly enough, for not attending synagogue, for eating non-kosher food. As she didn't want me in her kitchen, she had offered to provide all my meals; but we were a long tram-ride away from the town centre and I did not want to be committed to coming back for lunch. Because eating out was expensive, when it suited me I bought snacks to eat in my room; one morning while I was out she found evidence of it.

It was my room while I paid the rent, I argued, and she had no right to have gone into it in the first place. "You ought to be ashamed of yourself," she shouted at me, "a grown girl like you, unable to keep her room clean!" The accusation was justified: I so much did not want this place to be my home that I had not been able to make myself sweep it out.

When Walter arrived, a couple of hours later, I was still crying: at the thought of needing once again to find somewhere else to live.

He promised to find somewhere for me, and he did.

For the next three years, my room was one with a bay window on the top floor of an apartment house, with—just—a view of

The Meadows. It was large and pleasant and, when Walter found it—before I had found work—better than we could afford. It made me worth something, in my own eyes, to have such a room to live in. The time came when, after work, I could not bear to go back to it, but that was because I could not face being alone.

So hard was it for me to feel at home anywhere, it did not even occur to me that I could move the furniture about to suit me better until a visitor suggested it.

Shortly after I moved in, the flat, with its tenants, changed hands; from then on my landlady was Mrs. Stewart, a widow with three grown sons; the unmarried youngest who came home on leave was in the air force. Mrs. Stewart believed (had been told by the previous owner?) that Walter and I were Greeks; I feared that she would want Jews no more than she would want Germans and the longer I put off correcting her the more impossible it became for me to tell her the truth. It made me, all the years I was there, reluctant to enter into conversation with her.

But as a landlady she was good to me, for instance on one particularly cold evening she lit the coal fire to give my room time to warm up before I came home.

When Mr. Jackson had left me to mind the shop, I had, after selling sand-paper or hinges, written on the till slip a lesser amount of money than I had received and pocketed the difference; I had not done it often and the money I stole could not, altogether, have amounted even to one pound. I did it partly out of curiosity: to see if it could be done and got away with, and to find out what it felt like. Partly I was taking revenge on Mr. Jackson for treating me like a slave, though he treated his wife no better when she came in on market days, to help out. Partly what prompted me was the grudge I had against society and to break its rules felt as good as scratching an itch.

But the reason he gave for refusing me a reference was that I had not been with him long enough to prove myself—although after four weeks he had, as agreed, increased my wages.

About to leave, I felt bold enough to argue with him; nobody could have won an argument with that dour Scotsman.

At the Edinburgh labour exchange I was told that, without a reference, they could not send me to apply for a job; being sent by the labour exchange was in itself considered by prospective employers to be a recommendation. On the other hand, jobs of the sort I was now looking for were no longer freely advertised. I said, "My husband is a soldier," and remained standing there, waiting, until the clerk eventually copied out for me just one of all the addresses she had: I could see them. "It's the best job on offer," she said, and I could not tell if she was being sarcastic or if she meant to make certain that I would be turned away.

George Street runs parallel behind Princes Street; it is, or was in those days, mainly residential, with only a few, rather superior shops. Dymock and Howden, a few steps from the West End, had been a wine merchant's, distilling its own brand of whiskey and selling its own brand of cigarettes hand made on the premises. It had also sold delicatessen, and when war broke out, to oblige its customers, added mundane groceries. The two men who had started the shop, giving their names to it, being bachelors had bequeathed it to two of their employees, one of whom was the father of the two men who now owned it. Between these, a fine distinction was observed: James Macdonald, responsible for the shop, was addressed as "Jim" by us all; the elder brother, who had abandoned a career in law to take over the running of the business from his father, was addressed as "Mr. Ian."

When Walter had visited Whittingehame, and we had gone to the tower, the old woman who had shown us the museum-like quarters said to have been inhabited by Mary Queen of Scots: that had been the Macdonald brothers' grandmother.

Mr. Ian was a tall, slim man of about my father's age—he had served in the First World War—with greying hair combed straight back: as my father wore his, and fine brown eyes: like my father's. He was married, with two sons, one already in his teens, and a small daughter. He was the first man I encountered since my marriage who made me remember what the Irish Annie had said.

He had a large private office downstairs, off the shop and out of sight of it; there was also a downstairs office for the staff—mostly employees of long standing—who dealt with customers over the telephone; the cash-desk was at one end of it. All the additional paper work caused by the war was done upstairs, on an L-shaped wooden balcony overhanging the working area at the back of the shop. This used to be the tobacco department, of which only two women were left, making cigarettes for an elite; they had come as school-leavers and grown old in their jobs: that was the sort of business this was.

When I applied for the job, I was shown upstairs, where Mr. Ian was sitting at the first of a row of desks, right there with his employees. If I had been a wealthy customer he could not have greeted me more courteously. And I was altogether captivated when, looking at my papers, he pronounced my name as it should be pronounced, as I had not heard it pronounced in years except by Walter: he had served with the British Army of Occupation and been stationed not far from my home town. He questioned me about my background more than about my work experience. When I confessed that I knew little about bookkeeping, he said, "A girl like you will soon pick it up." It may be regarded as feudal, that we were all "girls" to him, but I preferred to see it as paternal. My wages would be thirty-five shillings. "Will you be able to manage on that?" he asked me. It was more than my weekly allowance as a soldier's wife. I had that, I explained, and was gratified to have been given this opportunity of demonstrating to him that not all Jews were rapacious.

He called Isobel over—either because she was also already married, or she may have been the nearest—and told her to befriend me. And she did.

The visitor who had suggested that I should move the furniture in my room was Kurt.

He was not the first friend whom Walter brought home with

him on a Saturday afternoon. There had been Hai, whom I had already met in Dumfries, and another man whose name I have forgotten. Before our marriage, Walter used to go about with these two; he talked of the three of them as "the triumvirate." Hai had become a corporal and Walter was by then a sergeant; his unit was still building camps and his promotion must have been due to his knowledge of his trade—I could not imagine him ordering people about, he was much too unassuming.

I had not taken to his friends and Walter, being blind (I believed) to my faults, blamed not my inability to relate to people but his choice of friends: they were not good enough to deserve me. He had first mentioned Kurt soon after I joined him in Scotland: there was this really, really interesting man in his unit, who under other circumstances would no doubt have been an officer; he was the only one of his comrades, Walter said, with whom it was possible to have a proper conversation—he meant one not about facts but ideas.

He felt flattered, he told me, that this man was seeking him out; had said in so many words that he wanted them to be friends; had arranged to share Walter's tent. Walter had said that he was just waiting for a suitable moment to invite him to meet me, when he stopped talking about him and started to make excuses: for someone like Kurt, the room I was living in wasn't good enough.

Walter believed that there were subjects about which a husband didn't talk to his wife, about which men didn't talk to women; homosexuality was one of them. Not that if he had done so I would at this time have understood what he meant.

Kurt believed that anything that could be thought could and probably ought to be said. He was to tell me that it was curiosity which had made him persuade Walter to invite him: he wanted to meet his rival for Walter's affection. At the last moment, he almost decided not to come because on the Friday he had broken a fingernail: that was why he then made an effort to be especially entertaining, to distract my attention from his broken fingernail. That was how he talked. He had rather ugly hands, with stubby fingers; looking at them I did not crave—as I did looking at Mr. Ian's hands—to be touched by them. I knew Kurt for more than a year before I began to be physically attracted to him, and then only because I had become emotionally enslaved. Kurt knew me heart and soul and understood me as no one, certainly not Walter, had ever done except my mother and Lise.

He was to say that it would have been more amusing—his word—if I had fallen in love with him, while he had continued to be in love with Walter, and Walter with me. But unexpectedly and against his will, at our first meeting he fell in love—which was always happening to him—but for the first time it was with someone of the other sex. And, being Kurt, he could not help setting about exploring the possibilities of such a relationship; he valued experience more than he valued anything else, more than even his own happiness.

He was about Walter's age, but seemed older to me because he was more mature and more intelligent than either of us, was better-educated and far better-read. He was taller than Walter, but held himself badly, and wasn't as muscular—had done no labouring before joining the army; but he had always practiced sport—tennis, swimming—enough to keep fit. He had black, very curly hair, prominent ears, a slightly curved nose and a thin-lipped, wide mouth. In fact he was ugly except for his piratical brown eyes.

My first memory of Kurt is of him sitting on the couch which stood in the bay window; neither Walter nor I had ever sat on it.

As it was not yet cold enough to sit by the fire, I must at the time have been married for about half a year. With his back to the window, so that I could not see the expression on his face—this would have been intentional—he talked of his arrest and his experiences in Buchenwald concentration camp. He had not talked about it before, ever; the after-effect was such that it made him stay away for weeks—while Walter and I wondered what we had done to upset him. When he came again, it was for the sake of checking his reaction to me: meanwhile he had persuaded himself that he had only imagined it. And was so disconcerted to find that he hadn't that Walter and I concluded that he wasn't well.

After this, he needed "of course" to come back in order to efface the bad impression he believed he had made on me, and to prove to himself that he remained in control; his repeated visits were "like probing a bad tooth," he was to tell me. At the time he joked about his reason for coming: all he wanted was to sit by my fire, or to drink mine rather than the NAAFI tea. He resorted to pretexts: he had something he wanted to give me; most often it was a book or books, he began to guide my reading. Sometimes it was chocolate, which he "couldn't trust Walter with," though he must have known that Walter, too, gave me his chocolate issue. I also got chocolate—and, once, a piece of the fresh salmon brought in by a customer—from Mr. Ian.

If I had been keeping a diary in Edinburgh, it would have included these entries:

— I have a room I like and a job I like in a place I like and I want to stay here. Walter has agreed that when he is posted elsewhere, as is bound to happen, I shan't have to move with him.

— If I can't live on my soldier's wife's allowance and save my wages, I shall live on my wages and save my allowance, against the end of the war. I have reopened my post office savings account with the eighteen pounds I have saved so far.

— I have joined the main public library in North Street. It has so many books I can't wait to read; I wish I could spend all my time reading. Now I can understand Anne's not wishing to be disturbed. That's one good thing about living on my own.

— I am sick of cooked food—or is it of English cooking? I've found a snack-bar where I can have a cheese sandwich and a piece of whatever cake is available and a cup of coffee all for one shilling. If that's all I want, Isobel commented when I told her, it would be cheaper to bring a packed lunch. It didn't occur to her that even I might still like to have things done for me even if I have to pay for it; she has lunch at her mother's.

Miss Mackay overheard us and told me that no restaurant is allowed to charge more than five shillings per person, and treated me to a meal at Gibson's in Princes Street, where we had a table with a view of the castle. I would have enjoyed the food more if I hadn't had to make conversation. In future I shall go there by myself, occasionally, as a treat.

— Isobel has the smallest of suitcases in which to carry her shopping. "So much smarter than a shopping-bag," she said, and I agree. I shall buy one like it.

— If I don't have to queue for too long for my food, then there is time enough left of my lunch-hour for me to do some shopping. But I do most of it on my way home on Saturdays, which is our half day. Meat is rationed by price: the better the cut, the less you get. My butcher allows me to save it up for the weekends when Walter comes home, so that I can make goulash—the only way I know how to cook meat. I don't bother cooking for myself; at most I heat a tin of baked beans. I like bread and cheese so much that it wouldn't bother me if I never had anything else. When my cheese ration runs out there's Spam, which I also like, to be had on points.

— One doesn't have to register for sweets, but I have difficulties getting my ration because shopkeepers keep things for their regular customers—meaning people who bought from them before ever I came to this country.

— I find it difficult to go into any place—to do anything for the first time. In a shop like Woolworth's you don't have to make yourself understood: you just take what you want and hold out the money. But Woolworth is right at the other end of Princes Street and it takes all my lunch-hour to walk there and back. I also like it because the lay-out is exactly as it was in Bielefeld. I am always reminded of Mutti chiding Lise and me for shopping in Woolworth; she used to say that it would shame us to be seen going in or out by people who knew us.

Looking for toothpaste, I was so pleased to see the familiar Odol! But then I saw that it said on the box, "British made for British teeth," and I didn't buy it.

— There must be Jews in Edinburgh; some of the men serving on the Whittingehame committee lived here. I haven't come across any and I don't much want to.

— It takes me twenty minutes to walk to work, which is no longer than I need to allow for taking the tram because of the waiting for it. And I prefer to walk, not only because it saves money. It's all the way either level or downhill, so walking home takes a little longer and I don't like doing it because of the blackout. Miss Young (one of the tobacco "girls"), who seems to hold me responsible for the sinking of British shipping by German U-boats, and means me whenever she talks about "people who've been with the firm no more than five minutes"—she's jealous because Mr. Ian lets me add up the Excise Book, which she isn't allowed to touch—keeps reminding her colleague of all the people who have been raped and/or killed in the course of the years while crossing The Meadows. There isn't a tram stop which would spare me doing that, and like everyone else I have only a small torch, taking a number eight battery—the only batteries one can get.

— Walter has bought me a second-hand gramophone, for five pounds. The records which came with it include one of Richard Tauber singing Schubert songs, and one of piano music by Chopin. I've been running home during my lunch-hour to listen, I'm enjoying it so much.

— The shop cat has had kittens, one totally black like the one I had as a child. They're in the basement; the people in the wine department who are looking after them said I was welcome to take one. I thought I'd better also ask Mr. Ian—an excuse for seeking him out in his private office. Mrs. Stewart (my landlady) said she didn't mind, that it could do its business in the coal cellar off the kitchen. I shall take it to bed with me, which is something Mutti didn't allow.

— I was listening to the shop-assistants talking about how they spend their evenings; one said, "By the time we're all home, and have had our tea, and cleared up, and done talking, it's already nearly bedtime." How strange to be living together with one's relations!

— Cinema-going has become an important part of my life. There are always lots of films to choose from and I don't mind taking the tram to the suburbs if there's something showing there which I want to see again. And I don't mind queuing. *Gone with the Wind* I can't watch often enough and I can see why it's popular. But there's something wrong with my taste because lots of films which I hear people raving about either bore me or leave me cold.

If I go straight from work instead of eating I'm not spending any more money. But I don't sit in the very cheapest seats: Mutti wouldn't approve of it.

— I'm not alone in my feelings: I've just read *Jane Eyre.*

— When the "Ration Girl" left, Mr. Ian gave me her job. Now I have a large desk round the corner from the cigarette-makers; it's almost like having my own office. I have to see that all the registered customers get what they are entitled to, neither more nor less; I hold the ration-books of those to whom we deliver and type out what rations are to be sent with their orders. I now have a typewriter at my disposal during my lunch-hour and after work.

— The shop floor—a mosaic of tiles, really rather special—has been dirty for days because the cleaning-woman is ill. I overheard Mr. Ian saying that he couldn't find anyone else and I offered to do it. He gave me a very strange look—no doubt he has forgotten that I was once a cleaning-woman at the ORT school. The bottle-washer from the wine department did it. I made my offer because I feel about the place just like the old people who've been here all their working lives; but Mr. Ian must have thought that I wanted the money: when I got my next pay-packet I discovered that he has increased my wages to two pounds.

— Mr. Ian received a phone-call in mid-morning, asking him to come to the school attended by his elder son. When he got there he was told that Hamish has been shot dead. He was fourteen years old. What happened was that another boy brought to school a revolver belonging to his father who is an officer on leave; he didn't realise that it was loaded and while he was showing it to his friends, it went off.

Mr. Ian took time off only to attend the funeral. He's wearing a black tie and a black armband but, judging by him, Scotsmen, as is said of Englishmen, don't show their feelings. It makes it impossible for anyone else—or only for me?—to show their feelings either.

— Walter and I went to London for part of his leave, staying in a bed-and-breakfast place run by refugees in Belsize Park. I'd looked forward to this visit for so long that, I suppose, it was bound to be disappointing. We met Hanne (the cousin whose mental breakdown had brought us together again); we had tea with her at the Lyons Corner House in Oxford Street. She's earning her living looking after somebody's children and said that the only thing wrong with her life now is that she hasn't got a boyfriend. We visited a Greek couple who befriended Walter when he was stationed in London. They are both working for the BBC and they made me realise that refugees don't inevitably have to be socially inferior. But then, these people have the advantage of not being Jews. I was impressed by Walter, by that they should have accepted him as a friend. They seemed to accept me, too; I hope that it didn't show that I felt so inferior to them.

I sought out the editor of the FDJ magazine, which was a waste of time because I don't really want still to get published in German, even if some of the time I am still writing in it. What I want to do with my writing is to make English people—I mean the people among whom I am living, people whose language is English—understand what it feels like to be me. When I said this to the editor of *Die Zeit*—the point of going to London was to meet him—he told me that if I wanted to write poetry in English, and express *myself,* be original, then the first thing I must do is to stop reading English poetry. I don't see how I can follow his advice: I'm very aware of my lack of education in general and particularly of not having had any English education. And I need poetry in my life and haven't yet got enough English to produce my own—what I write in that language are no more than exercises. But at least he didn't tell me that I won't be able to do it.

— Because I get so much pleasure out of the gramophone, in spite of having only a few records, Walter suggested buying a wireless: as a soldier's wife I am allowed to have one. They're hard to find second-hand. I mentioned it to Mr. Ian, who mentioned it to someone else, and on Saturday afternoon Walter and I went to collect one from Corstorphine. We paid sixteen pounds for it.

Now I run home at lunch-time to hear what's on, and in the evenings I'm staying in to listen. It makes me want to do more knitting than I have coupons to buy wool with. Some time ago, I came across a pattern for a toy dog, and bought it, because I liked the look of it so much, and there are yarns which are not soft enough to use for jumpers which can be bought without coupons.

Not knowing what to do with the dog after I had made it, I offered it to the Binns toy department and they bought it for seven shillings; I later saw it on display in the window priced one guinea. Still, it earned me a little and I had fun making it, so I shall do some more, cats as well, which they said they would buy if they were ready before Christmas.

— I've discovered that if I buy a skirt in a children's department I have to give up fewer coupons for it. And it doesn't need shortening. My waist-measurement is twenty and a half inches.

— I'm very bad at getting up in the mornings. Another thing I'm bad at is cleaning my room. One Sunday morning when I had my period and felt bad enough to stay in bed, Walter swept the floor and ever since—remembering what happened in my previous digs—when he stays he's the first to get up on a Sunday morning and does the weekly cleaning before I get out of bed.

— Because of my constant headaches I finally went to the oculist—everybody said I should go. So now I wear glasses for reading and writing. (I didn't really need them and later dispensed with them.) Mr. Ian noticed me wearing them; he came back to tell me that he's only just realised that all his "girls" upstairs are wearing glasses. He straight away arranged to have fluorescent lighting installed.

— As I was walking past Binns to see if my dog had been sold, I heard my name being called: it was Karl-Heinz, our Whittingehame star footballer. He's an apprentice engineer in Rugby and up here on a visit. He's staying quite centrally with a Miss Johnson, who lets rooms to foreign students; he was surprised that I hadn't heard of her. He's such a good mixer that he can't understand people who aren't.

He called for me after work to introduce me at Miss Johnson's. Is she a rich woman who has fallen on hard times, or does she offer a home to young men without family out of the goodness of her heart, or does she do it out of loneliness? She's middle-aged, and what Mutti would call *gebildet* (cultured); a gentlewoman. We all had tea together, off fine china held on our laps, in her sumptuous sitting-room.

In Tom I have again met someone who reminded me of what the Irish Annie said; he's a medical student who came here years before the war, to finish his schooling. He said that his father, who is a doctor, was far-sighted. He has his younger brother with him; their parents are still in Hungary. He has very white skin with an abundance of freckles, coarse curly black hair, and eyes the colour of beech leaves in autumn.

Miss Johnson invited me to have lunch with her later in the week—so that we can get to know each other, she said.

— I've become friendly with Margaret, a new girl at work. I don't know quite why—she's very religious—we just seem to like each other. She's about my age, a Girl Guide and the leader of a Brownie pack. Her father walked out on them while her mother was in hospital, giving birth to her. The flat they live in comes with her mother's job as housekeeper; she took me home:

that's the second flat I've been into as a visitor, in Edinburgh. No, the third: Isobel took me home once; somehow she and I have remained no more than acquaintances.

— Tom's brother Walter is studying to be a veterinary surgeon. I went with the two of them to the home of a dentist from Vienna; Walter was to trim their cat's claws. I mentioned that I've been attending the free clinic, staffed by dental students—I'm having a lot of trouble with my teeth. Mr. Hegemann offered to treat me, at a discount.

— A very pretty girl—she can't be much older than I—holds a weekly poetry reading in the basement part of one of the Princes Street bookshops. It was attended mainly by elderly women. She read romantic poems by Keats and other known poets, as well as her own work, which is on sale in home-made, handwritten pamphlets. She manages to make her poems sound a lot better than they are. I don't want to have written her poems, but I'd rather be her than me.

— Margaret borrowed for me the *Collected Poems of Wilfred Owen* from her branch of the public library; it isn't in mine and it's also not available in the shops. I am copying the whole of the book out, so that I can read these poems whenever I want to; some of them I already know by heart. I can't remember how I discovered him and Siegfried Sassoon—whose *Selected Poems* are on sale; I've bought a copy—I feel as if I had always known them. I relate to them and therefore I feel related.

Query: does this mean that I ought to be a pacifist?

I've read Sassoon's *The Complete Memoirs of George Sherston.* There doesn't seem to be any book on the life of Wilfred Owen; I am thinking about writing one. I've written to Edmund Blunden (*Undertones of War*), who edited the *Collected Poems,* and to Sassoon, to enquire if they are willing to help me with information.

I've got Mr. Ian's permission to stay in the shop after closing time to use the typewriter, as often and for as long as I like.

— I went to a meeting of something calling itself "The Writers' Group." Most of the people there were elderly women.

I overheard them asking each other, "Are you working on anything?" and answering that there was always too much else to do. Amateurs all; I don't belong with them and I shan't go again.

— If I believed in omens, I would think it one that Wilfred Owen spent some time in Edinburgh. The *Scotsman* printed my letter asking for information and I went to interview a woman who used to visit him while he was in the Craiglockhart hospital.

— Both Blunden and Sassoon have answered my letters. Blunden says that if I send him what I have written he will comment on it. According to Sassoon, what matters is not the life of the poet but the poems. That's like saying that it's the apples that matter and not the apple-tree.

(I was too ignorant to know how to collect the necessary material and had to abandon the project.)

Having such minimal contact with people in what were for me formative years, of course books influenced me. Round Miss Johnson's tea-table on a Sunday afternoon, discussions ranged wide and once, when I voiced my opinion, Tom asked me, teasingly, "What book have you been reading lately?" thus making me aware of it.

Still at school in Germany, when I was fourteen, studying the *Antigone* by Sophocles, I came across her words, "I exist not to participate in hating but in loving," and instantly chose them to be one of my maxims. But if I had, before reading Owen and Sassoon, come across moral arguments against the waging of war, I had not taken them in; I had been unaware that there were any, had accepted warfare as part of the human condition. I grew up knowing that during the First World War my father had served for four years in the German trenches, and in my last years at home, my mother used to say that only a war would be able to get rid of Hitler. Of course I was against Hitler, not only because he was an enemy of the Jews but because of all he stood for. But the issue was confused for me precisely by my Jewishness; I knew that identifying with the causes of the countries in which they happened to be living had in the past made Jews fight against each other. I knew that, had it not been for Hitler's attitude to the Jews, there would now be also Jews fighting as German nationals for Germany. I knew what the self-styled Free World was fighting against; I also knew that freedom within it was limited and that in parts of it the people were not free at all. And I didn't know what it was fighting *for.*

Besides all the generally valid arguments in favour of the pacifism which reading Owen and Sassoon had caused me to adopt, it allowed me to avoid taking sides: against the country which my father had fought for, and for the country which was being fought against by the Jews in the Land of Israel. Though originally, when the question had arisen a year and a half before, while I was living in Leeds, my reasons for wanting to join the ATS had not been abstract but selfish, as had those which had made me decide against joining up.

When there was a rumour that soldiers' wives without children not engaged in war work were also to be called up, I mentioned to Margaret that I was considering declaring myself to be a conscientious objector. Mr. Ian happened to be sitting at his desk upstairs and overheard me. He told me that I was not to do that: if necessary he would be able to get me exempted on the grounds that, as the "Ration Girl," I was one of his key workers.

What was wrong with my marriage was that Walter could not manage to make me feel loved. Perhaps it could not be done: not my father, not Anne, but only my mother and Lise had ever made me feel loved, and now I felt that I was unlovable because my emotions reacted to my having had to leave home as if my mother had rejected me, and to Lise being sent away as if she had deserted me. But both my father and Anne had, at least sometimes, made me feel valued.

Walter could not manage to make me feel valued because he was so unassuming that he was unable to think much of the girl who had married him. Which was the mirror-image of how I felt about him; perhaps we were too alike to be good for each other, to be able to help each other.

Perhaps I had never loved him for himself but had loved only his familiarity. I assume that he loved me better than I loved him because I was the one who ended the relationship, long after I had begun to want to end it. He tried again and again, for years he tried to dissuade me. Or perhaps he found it even harder than I to cope with another loss.

He was old-fashioned enough to see women in general as inferior to men and that was how I saw them, too. I needed a husband I could look up to and though I did not allow myself to realise it at the time, evidently I was ashamed of him, or perhaps what I was ashamed of was myself in his presence. I never once took him with me to Miss Johnson's; I went to her occasionally during the week for lunch, and on a Saturday or a Sunday afternoon when Walter remained in camp. Whenever he was on leave I took time off work; but there were occasions when he waited for me outside the shop, and I saw him waiting, and did not call him in to introduce him to Mr. Ian. None of the people I was beginning to know ever met him. He was not interested in meeting them. Perhaps he believed that his "little woman" was capable only of associating with the sort of people I had fallen among in Bradford.

There were things about Walter which I had always disliked, and been aware of disliking. He was small for a man, as I am small for a woman. As the youngest of three sisters I was—still am—sensitive about this; I objected to any inference that I must therefore be a lesser person also in non-physical respects. Walter had talents: he could play the piano almost as well as Lise, he could draw and paint as well or better than I; he even occasionally wrote poetry, and though I didn't think much of it, I thought that perhaps I was wrong because once, during those years when nothing of mine got published, one of his poems got published in the *Observer.* But he always referred to himself as "little me." And to me he usually referred as "my little woman."

There were subjects—religion, Zionism—about which he had thought long and hard and arrived at conclusions. He expected me, as his wife, to accept his opinions, expected me to let him, as my husband, do my thinking for me. "Don't you bother your pretty little head about it," he would say, when I tried to discuss, for instance, ideas of philosophy about which I had been reading. "You'll get wrinkles," he would say when I frowned, as if that were what mattered, and run his fingertips across my forehead. Nobody except my parents and sisters had ever touched me so matter-of-factly and that he had the right to do so made his touch obnoxious to me.

As far as our sex life was concerned, we were too ignorant and too inhibited to advance from the basics. Perhaps if we had had a normal married life the monotony of it would have driven us to experimentation. But throughout eighteen months of constant separations, to be together again was always physically so comforting that it felt like enough. In time, his routine love-making began to bore me, leave me unsatisfied. My mother had let me go out into the world without explaining sex to me because she was unable to talk about it. I was unable to talk about it, too.

I had become a compulsive knitter: knitting a pullover for myself was one childhood ambition which circumstances had left within my reach. When I didn't have the clothing coupons to buy more wool, I unraveled what I had knitted some months or even only weeks before, to knit up again differently. Finding new stitches and designing styles provided some outlet for my need to be creative.

I was using, for the first time, a Fair Isle pattern, to knit a jumper, in what was in those days called nigger-brown, to match my hair, with multi-coloured stripes; I did not like it when it was finished, but I found the making of it engrossing. I was counting my stitches, not really paying attention to what Kurt was saying; he liked to hear the sound of his own voice and I often felt that he was talking for his own benefit more than mine. I didn't mind that: I found his mere company pleasing.

That Saturday afternoon he had turned up by himself, saying that Walter—whom I had been expecting—was unable to come and had sent him along in his stead. It was still cold enough for me to have lit the fire: it must have been the fourth spring of the war, when I had been married for not much more than a year. I had two bulky armchairs, permanently on either side of the fire-place; Kurt had been sitting opposite me but now he was standing, steadying one elbow on the mantelpiece, the other hand in his pocket, probably shaking. He was not nearly as sure of himself, confronted with his feelings about me, as he was at all other times and as he managed to make me believe. He was a heavy smoker; now he was chain-smoking.

I heard him say, "Wouldn't it be regrettable if your husband were to walk in through that door at this moment?" It made me glance over my shoulder at the door.

I rested my hands in my lap and looked up at him. I asked him, "Why do you say that?" my formula for when I hadn't been listening properly or not understood him; I was—still am—a bad listener.

"Don't you think you and I are getting on better without him?"

I wondered what he had been saying while I had been counting stitches.

Until I changed it some years after the war, my name was Kate, pronounced in German as two syllables. My family had hardly ever used it; especially my mother and Lise had a variety of pet names for me, the one they had used most often had been *Kätze,* a cross between the German for cat and for kitten. It was Kurt who named me Kat. Frau Kat was what he called me, the Frau standing for more than Mrs., as any German word we used always stood for more than itself. And because I was only nineteen and still looked like a schoolgirl, it always sounded to me as if he were implying that I was far from being a "little woman": that I was somebody to be reckoned with, a challenge—as, of course, I was to him, and I realised it, long before I understood why I was that.

He must have begun to manipulate my mind—he used to say that that was what he was doing, called himself, signed his letters to me, "your bad influence"—almost as soon as we met: with the book-token, worth five shillings, which Anne sent me for my birthday in 1942, I bought the *Collected Works of Oscar Wilde,* printed on fine paper and bound in leather; I still have it. I remember buying it. Wilde was popular in Germany, Lise had had a collection of his stories suitable for children; but my choice was a gesture of goodwill towards Kurt.

That Saturday afternoon was the first time we were alone together; afterwards I suspected him of having engineered this opportunity for himself, he was quite capable of doing so—not out of malice towards Walter but out of pure selfishness. He warned me, repeatedly, that he came first with himself, that I must beware of him if I did not want to get hurt; I believe that to begin with he loved me enough to want to spare me his problems, and that later he loved me so much that he wanted me to help him solve them.

Or so he said, and I believed him: I always did; I was at the mercy of his sophistication. On that Saturday afternoon, having succeeded in making me lose interest in my knitting, he leant forward and kissed me on the forehead. Then he straightened up, with the grin of a child who believes he has done something clever, and lit himself another cigarette.

He had taken me completely by surprise: it had not occurred to me that he might be interested in me in *that* way. I thought of my body, its looks, as something for which I could take no credit, and therefore appreciation of it could not feed my pride, not combat my sense of inferiority: only approval of my mind could do that, because I thought of its quality as being: within my conscious control. I had believed that it was my mind Kurt was interested in, that he had got into the habit of visiting for the sake of talking with me. That, before this, something had been going on within him which had been inhibited by the presence of Walter, he had managed altogether to conceal from me.

It was all right for the Irish Annie, I thought, to leave her husband because the world was full of other men whom she liked better. My dissatisfaction with Walter was no greater or stronger than my dissatisfaction with myself; I thought that we were about right for each other, that I could not aspire to someone like, for instance, Tom.

While I believed that what drew Kurt to me was a sexual attraction, I remained unaffected; I felt that it was an affront to my intelligence that he should seek me out for the sake of my flesh. But once he had got me to understand that, on the contrary, physically he found me—his word—unappetising, and that what he valued me for was the sort of person I was, I was eager to be his ally in the war he was fighting against himself, not caring much about the consequences to Walter and our marriage.

Anne's Death–End of the War

(Edinburgh)

When I returned from Bristol after Anne's death, Walter was waiting for me at the station. Perhaps my letter to him had said that I would be travelling overnight to arrive on Monday morning and perhaps there was only the one train which could have brought me back: what I remember is writing to him in so many words that I did not want him to meet me. I needed time, in the familiar surroundings of Edinburgh, which I had come to love and to think of as home, to accommodate the thought of Anne being dead, my memories of her, her soul—partly for Anne's sake and partly for mine: what I was bringing back with me was the luggage of her death.

And there was Walter waiting to greet me as if I were returning from some jaunt, smiling his apologetic smile as if he had the right to count on being forgiven for having ignored my wish, as if he could count on my agreeing with him that he knew what I wanted, knew what was good for me, better than I did myself. As if what had happened in Bristol had happened only to Anne and not also to me. As if the meaning of everything, as if my perception of life itself had not changed. Asking me, "Aren't you glad to see me, glad to be back?" Putting his arms about me as if he owned me, calling me "little *Kätze*" as if this hybrid of my childhood name had healing powers, when I didn't want to be healed because that would have meant being unfaithful to Anne, deserting her, being reconciled to the decay of her in her grave. What have I done, I thought, to have granted this outsider entry into my family life—"my family" meaning for me then and for years to come—until *after* the birth of the four children I was to have by another husband—the family I had come from. The thought of it more important to me than ever now that it was no longer whole except in my mind.

I wished Walter away: out of my presence, away from Edinburgh, out of my life. I needed someone, he was right about that, saying, "You'll have to make do with little me." Did he believe, genuinely believe, believe for one moment, that he could take Anne's place with me, fill up the crater which her death had left in my life? How could he possibly believe that when he had known her, knew what she had been like; when he knew me—and if he didn't know, understand me better than that, what was he doing walking beside me with his arm about my waist, being my husband?

I needed someone but it wasn't him. How preferable, how much more satisfactory, I thought, it would have been if the soldier waiting for me at the station barrier had been Kurt. He was the one whom I wanted to be with, whose presence would—not have comforted, consoled me: I didn't want to be consoled, there was no consolation for Anne's death. But I could have talked to him, he would have listened, he would have known what to say, known how to make me feel understood and therewith to feel less alone.

That was the moment when I realised that I loved Kurt.

It was important to him, in view of the feelings he had once had for Walter, to know that he was not responsible for the break-up of our marriage: it left me with Kurt, all I wished for, but Walter it left with no one. It was important to me as well to know it: a woman whose reason for leaving her husband was love for another man I thought of as a whore.

It was because I found talking with Kurt preferable to talking with Walter that I preferred being with him. Apart from shaking hands according to the convention of the country we had come from, and apart from the kiss which Kurt had planted on my forehead the first time we had been alone, there was no touching between us, until after Anne's death.

Not until the spring, March or April, did Walter accept that I meant it when I said that I wanted no longer to be married to him. By then he was stationed a long way away from Edinburgh; he had transferred from the Pioneer Corps to the Royal Engineers, and anglicised his name in anticipation of the Allied landings in Normandy. Throughout that winter, he still came "home"—home having been each for the other rather than my room—and I was not able to stop him, did not really want to stop him, because where else could he have gone? What I felt for him now was pity, because of the predicament I was putting him in, especially now when he was about to go on active service; but I thought it also immoral to dissemble. For the sake of our past life together, out of gratitude to him, I agreed to go on as before, have him come for weekends to be with me, since it meant so much to him: more than it meant to me to be free of him. We had only the one bed: it meant sharing it, and since it meant so much to him I let him do as he wished; our love-making had from the first been something he did to me rather than something we did together. He wanted to do it more than I did not want him to; I had got used to it and the truth is that I also needed the comfort of touch. All the more so as my relationship with Kurt was still chaste.

"Haven't I been a good husband to you?" Walter asked me, and the answer was yes, he had been that. Within his limitations: but I could not manage to put into words what these were. "Is there anyone else?" he asked me, knowing that there was Kurt, and believing that he knew enough about him, and enough about me, to see the relationship between Kurt and me as no threat to our marriage. "I don't need to find someone else to love before I can stop loving you," I told him, and though under the circumstances it was a misleading statement—and was intended to mislead—it was also true.

It was also true, as Walter said, that I was still upset about Anne's death—I was to remain upset about it for the rest of my life. And Anne's death did have something to do with the break-up of our marriage: less because, on the Monday morning in Bristol, Walter had fucked me against my will than because Anne's death made me question the meaning of life.

It had more to do with Anne's death than with what feelings I had for Walter that, during the early weeks of my bereavement, I decided that what I wanted was to have a child. I wanted to become pregnant, and give birth to a girl, and call her Anne. And I would exchange my room for a small unfurnished flat, and make a real home for my baby and its parents. I lay awake at night planning how, in spite of the blackout, I would be able both to keep a window open for the healthy development of her lungs and to switch on a light so that I could attend to my Anne when she cried. I persuaded a shopkeeper to sell me some baby wool, of a quality available only to holders of babies' clothing coupons; I hadn't got mine yet, I said, but I was pregnant: believing that I was, because Walter and I had had intercourse without the use of condoms and my period was overdue.

It would have suited Kurt. He did not want me to leave Walter, told me, "Let him keep your body, it's of no use to me." His crudeness was intended to disenchant me; appalled to be experiencing a young man's normal physical reactions, he was trying to make me reject him. The situation demanded of me a maturity which I had not known I had; exercising it made me feel good about being who I was, enhancing my feelings for Kurt, who was responsible for this.

As suddenly as the wish to bear a child had come to me, it was annulled by a revulsion against the idea one afternoon as I was sitting at my desk and Isobel came to say something to me; she was about eight months pregnant. "It's perfectly understandable," Kurt reassured me. "You want to have relations but you know that they can die and therefore you don't want to risk it."

I always accepted as true whatever he said to me. He must

have been able to see more clearly than I did, at the time, that I had become much less concerned with life than with death.

The cinema was my refuge; even on the Friday and the Saturday between Anne's death and her funeral, at a loss what to do, I had considered going to the cinema—any cinema, to see any film; what had stopped me was what I had thought of as the possibility that Anne would know it, and disapprove. It felt to me as if her spirit, her soul were still about; I felt its presence, like an incorporeal moth, when I was alone in my room. That autumn, instead of going to the cinema after work so as to escape solitude, I hurried home, to be by myself and feel the presence of Anne.

I experienced it most strongly then, when I could concentrate on it. I thought that perhaps my concentrating on it obliged her soul to present itself to me and this was what frightened me: that what I thought and what I felt might make a difference to what survived of Anne: that her immortal soul was at my mercy. How was I to know what would have pleased her better: to be kept in my company or to be let go? I pleaded with what survived of her—it was as if I were praying to her—to dictate to me, as she had done in life, what I should do and think and feel that would guarantee me her approval, which was what I had most wanted while she was alive, and even now there was nothing I wanted more. That something of her survived I did not doubt: I had no experience of the world without Anne, and could not yet face it.

I did not know what Jews believe about death, and did not try, did not want to find out for fear that it would not suit me. I had a suspicion that the image of God on his throne surrounded by jubilating angels, which had been foisted on me when I was a child, was really more a part of Christian mythology; I did not think that it was reconcilable with the Old Testament figure of Yahweh.

I could not—I still can't—understand why those who believe that this life is no more than a prelude to a better one agree with unbelievers that dying must be delayed for as long as possible and that the dead are to be mourned instead of envied. I questioned Margaret, the Girl Guide I had made friends with in the office. She was in her early twenties and in indifferent health and told me that she hoped to die before she was thirty so as to be still at her best when she came into the presence of Jesus. She was a Congregationalist and suggested that I should attend a church service with her, and meet her minister.

I had been inside churches, occasionally, to look at the architecture, but more for the experience of seeing the light coming in through stained glass windows—something for which I have always had a minor passion. In Catholic churches I had looked at the images of the crucified Christ and wondered how people could worship a God they conceived of as merciful through this symbol of human suffering, and why the memory of one tortured Jew should have become an age-long incitement to a world-wide hatred of his people.

But I was not searching for any God: what I was searching for was contact with the soul of my dead sister. The Jewish prayer for the dead does no more than affirm the justice of God and the meaningfulness of life. Having grown up in a Christian environment, I was aware that Christianity offers to mourners more comfort and hope (one of the reasons why it instead of Judaism was adopted by the pagan Romans). I did go to church with Margaret, but only once and not until after I had been to a study-group meeting with her and met the minister. He was an imposing-looking, very vital young man, about to go out to Madagascar as a missionary. I liked him, and I liked the atmosphere of the study-group meeting, reminiscent of the weekly Bible class I had attended in the year before Hitler came to power: out of nostalgia, I continued to attend it. Once, I went on an outing into the Pentland Hills with this group of young Christians as if I—used to doing things mostly on my own—were one of them. But like so much else during these apprentice years, this involvement was something I had started for the wrong reason and after a while it was a relief to put a stop to it.

I also tried to make contact with Anne's soul by means of the occult. Through books I found in the library, I discovered that there were people who claimed to be able to communicate with the dead. Once I had become aware of their existence, they seemed to be everywhere. I saw an advertisement for a seance to be held in the Usher Hall and went to it. Every seat was filled and it felt good to me to be among people who all wanted the same thing I did: to hear the name of the one for whom we were mourning called out, by a slight middle-aged man, with the spotlight on him, moving urgently about the stage, his hands reaching out as if for something visible only to him. Names were what he plucked from the air, of sons or brothers or husbands or boyfriends who had died or been killed in one of the many theatres of war or as prisoners of the Germans or of the Italians or of the Japanese. And, always, out of the darkened auditorium someone responded, supplementing the personal details put forward by the medium until the identification was no longer in doubt, and, every time, through the medium, the dead reassured and consoled the living.

I had not expected Anne's soul to lend itself to such a public display and so was not disappointed. The next day, during my lunch-hour, I went to where the medium was staying—a modest hotel—and booked a private seance for an evening later that week.

I was not so gullible, so blinkered by my feelings, that it did not occur to me that there was time for the medium to have his helpers make enquiries about me—but who could have told him much? I could neither eat nor sleep, could barely do my work, so churned up within was I in anticipation of being vouchsafed a glimpse of the far side of death. If Anne was blissful in her new state, I would join her. Provided she wanted me to: I must make sure of the presence of mind to find out.

If something of her had indeed survived, it would have been out of character for her to have responded to the medium's summons, or she would have done so only to be angrier with me than I had ever made her in life. I realised this as I was shown into the room in which the seance was to be held, and lacked the self-assurance to call it off although it needed more courage to go through with it. Would I prefer to have the lights dimmed, or not? the man asked me. "Leave them on, please," I said, and with that perhaps made it inevitable that nothing he was going to say would make much of an impression on me, and perhaps the man knew it and that made what followed merely banal. Ashamed of myself for having adulterated what I saw at the time as the most important relationship in my life, of having involved a stranger in it out of greed, out of a youngest child's need for more, I tried not to listen, not to memorise what the medium was saying, not even for the purpose of discussing it with Kurt, as I did everything. The sense I had had of Anne's immanence drained out of me; I let it go because I thought that I did not deserve it.

And only then did I realise that it had been a burden to me.

After the funeral, the two ATS girls had asked me, concerning Anne's belongings, did I want them to sort through them, and let me have whatever was worth sending; Anne had never thrown anything away, not even chocolate wrappers, they told me. I did not want strangers to handle her belongings; I knew that she would not have liked it; I asked them just to parcel everything up. I knew that she would not have liked me to go through her belongings either; I intended just to keep everything that had been hers until I could give it to our mother, after the war.

But when her things, two small parcels, arrived, it was obvious to me that their contents had been selected: it included nothing that could simply be thrown away. Since other people had looked through her papers, I felt entitled also to look through them, and learned that the rest of her belongings—all her civilian clothes—were stored in a London warehouse. I wrote to claim them.

One day in November, when I came home from work, I found a familiar trunk bearing our father's initials, and a leather suitcase which had belonged to our grandfather. Having, when I had moved from Nanclwyd Lodge to Leeds, been reduced to owning no more than the clothes I was wearing and a change of underwear, two or three weeks before clothes rationing was introduced, I had expected to be delighted to get her things. Throughout my childhood, I had preferred her cast-offs to something of my own choice new from the shops.

It had not occurred to me, before I opened the cases, that they would contain all unfamiliar clothing, things which she had acquired since coming to England which I had never seen her wear—the sight of which served only to make me realise what a stranger she had become to me during the years of our separation: all her belongings were those of a stranger.

And then, as I turned the things over, wondering what to do with them, I came across an apron, a rectangle not much bigger than a tea-cloth with straps to tie round the waist, of seersucker cotton with thin multi-coloured criss-cross stripes. I had believed that only Lise and I had owned those and my first thought was that it must have belonged to Lise. My second thought was: now I don't mind having lost Anne since it has led to my getting this.

After that, all I wanted was to rid myself, quickly, totally, of everything I had inherited. Her clothes I gave away to charity; her books I gave as presents to Tom and his brother and other German-speaking students at Miss Johnson's. I burned her papers from a correspondence course on draughtsmanship which she had been taking, my letters and old letters from our parents: from our mother with our father's signature. There were some small wooden ornaments, assorted animals, which she had valued enough to bring with her out of Germany. Though I had always been forbidden to touch her belongings, on the day and the days after the synagogues burned, I carried some of these animals about in my pockets, not knowing what might be done in our absence to our home: so much had I cherished them. I kept them for Lise, and gave them to her at our first reunion, eight years after our separation, two years after the end of the war.

The post did not arrive until after I had left for work. Now when I hurried home during my lunch-hour, it was to look if there was a letter from Kurt; just to see his handwriting—crabbed as Anne's had been—made me feel euphoric. I wrote to him almost every day; I wrote poems to him as I had once done to Pummi. He frequently wrote to me. He came to see me whenever he could, though most of his leaves he spent in London, where he had relations, whose goodwill mattered to him because, unlike me, he was already making long-term plans for his life after the war.

Walter and I continued to exchange letters. In the early spring he met—as soldiers in wartime met wealthy women doing voluntary welfare work—Ursula Waley, the sister of the poet Lascelles Abercrombie and sister-in-law of the translator of poems from the Chinese. She invited him to spend his next leave at her home in Somerset.

I was invited as well, he wrote to me. I wrote back that I did not want to join him: I knew what would happen if I did. There was by now a physical dimension to my relationship with Kurt and I did not want to be shared. Walter still believed that, as he had once told me, Kurt was someone whom a man could trust with his wife.

For the next month or so, we exchanged letters, each saying that the other needed the holiday more and was the one who should go to Somerset. I felt guilty about depriving Walter, until he wrote that he had promised my parents to look after me and that that was what he was doing by providing for me, at last, a proper holiday. Followed almost immediately by another letter announcing that his leave had been cancelled.

A Visit to Mrs. Waley

The journey, on the first Friday in May, right across England, requiring two changes, and made in wartime, had been exhausting for the young foreigner—for more than two years a married woman but, with her hair loose about her shoulders, no make-up, and in her simple clothes, she looks like a schoolgirl. Dusk is falling; supposing Mrs. Waley has not come to the station in Taunton to meet her as her letter said she would? What would she do then? Is this visit going to be worth all the anxiety it has already cost her? What is the good of asking herself that now that she has come?

A gaunt woman, not as old as she looks to this girl, nor as hideously painted and adorned as she looks in this light, pounces, snatches one of her hands and will not let it go. The first thing she says is, "How clever of you to have blue eyes with dark hair! Oh, those eyes, they're gorgeous! Walter has got himself a little beauty!" The girl knows that she isn't that, though her eyes—not blue but grey—have been commented on before: some boys at her boarding school called her "the cat with the cow-eyes." She thinks Mrs. Waley favours hyperbole—a word she knows how to spell but not how to pronounce, like other words which she has come across only in her reading.

Mrs. Waley's house is an old one which has been modernized; it is full of antique furniture and of ornaments. It stands in its own extensive grounds. Mrs. Waley apologises for the condition of the house and garden and explains that the war has left her with only one maid and a part-time gardener. "Do you know how to garden?" she asks the girl in the course of the evening, and also says, "I'm learning to iron my blouses myself. Do you do your own blouses?" The girl thinks that she might easily have been in this house as a servant instead of as a guest. That this thought does not upset but amuse her is proof that she has come far since her servant days. For that she has to thank Miss Johnson, Mr. Ian, Tom, and above all Kurt, who keeps telling her that he is a bad influence. The thought of him, of her love for him, his love for her, makes her smile.

"You should smile more often," Mrs. Waley says. "When you smile you look beautiful."

There are six bedrooms; she is shown into one of them by Mrs. Waley, who asks her if it will do. The girl thinks that it will make her dream that she is a princess, and it won't be altogether a dream: she is being treated like one. There are other houseguests: an elderly painter and an army major, who are living here; a weekend visitor, an American soldier, is expected to arrive in the morning.

Mrs. Waley tells the girl that she is to share her own bathroom, shows it to her: it is covered, walls and ceiling, with pale blue tiles, and the bath is sunk into the floor and black with golden fittings; she has never seen anything so royal even in a film. It doesn't occur to her that she is to share it because the other visitors are male; she thinks that Mrs. Waley is treating only her as an equal.

She thinks that if her husband had come, together they would not have made such a good impression on their hostess.

The American soldier turns out to be another refugee: the scion of a Jewish banking house Aryanised by the Nazis; the whole family managed to escape to New York. He is a well-grown, good-looking young man, a major in the Intelligence Corps—so he says: there is no indication of rank on his uniform. Asked about it, he explains that this is so that he can assume a rank superior to the one of any man he may have to interrogate. The natives—in this case including the girl—don't know whether or not to believe him. To them, everybody in American uniform looks like an officer.

His name is Karl Victor Hagen; he tells them to address him as KV. The girl surmises that Mrs. Waley doesn't much like him: to the taste of a member of the English upper class he is too sure of himself. The girl thinks that she could fall in love with him if she weren't in love with another, until he asks her, "How come that your parents didn't know that they ought to leave Germany?"

The question instantly makes her heart bring her blood to the boil. Of course they knew that; there was not a country in the world willing to have them. This is literally true: she helped her father, over the years, to post letters of application to embassies, organisations, individuals, in many countries on every continent.

"They should have been able to get out," KV says, "other people did, and not only those who had money." He is quite unaware that he has upset her: after five and a half years among the British, she has learned not to show it. She wonders if, indeed, her parents are to blame, wonders about it not for the first time but only briefly; this is not the moment to think about it, KV is merely making conversation.

Their hostess, trying to mediate between her guests, tells him that the girl is interested in poetry. The girl thinks that "interest" is not the word for it: poetry crouches at the core of her life. But she believes that one cannot say of one-self that one is a poet; all one can say is that one writes—if one does—poetry. And for the time being she is between languages, and does not want to be told, yet again, that one has to be born to a language in order to be able to write poems in it. Thinking about this and, at the same time, trying to keep up her end of the conversation, to show that she is not ignorant she mentions Yeats. Those hearing her exchange looks. She has pronounced the name to rhyme with Keats, whom she has heard spoken of; it so happens that nobody has yet spoken to her of Yeats.

There are other embarrassing moments. For instance, at one of the meals—the cooking is excellent, the servings are frugal—asparagus is being served; the girl has not eaten it since early childhood. She eats it all up before she realises that everyone else has eaten only the tips and left the stalks.

On Sunday morning, while the Gentiles are attending church, the two Jews take a walk together. The sun is shining, the birds are singing, the trees and bushes are in new leaf and there are spring flowers in the hedgerows. It does not do to let one's thoughts dwell on the war (which will last for another full year) and at this moment one could easily forget it. The girl is dressed from the skin up in new clothes bought especially for this holiday; her blouse, from the Jaeger shop in Princes Street, is an expensive one with a paisley pattern which she has long coveted. Her flared grey flannel skirt comes from the children's department in the basement of C & A. Her shoes are brown brogues. Because of the war, it is all right to go without stockings and the still-fresh morning air reaching her bare thighs reminds her of the spring days of her childhood, when one could first leave off the liberty bodice that went with the long woollen stockings; it reminds her of the sudden sense of freedom this used to give her. Then it meant getting out the skipping rope. And what does it mean now?

The American soldier is more than a head taller than she in spite of her medium-high heels; she has, literally, to look up to him. Only making conversation, he says, "I am sorry not to meet your husband."

The girl has a physical sensation akin to that of swallowing a too-hot drink too quickly. When this has passed, she says, I, I, I'm going to get a divorce. She has been moving towards this decision since her sister's death and has arrived at it now by telling it to someone.

"What's wrong with him?" KV asks, lightly. "Does he treat you badly?"

She explains that he is a very nice young man but not right for her—or rather, she tries to explain to herself as well as to him what she has not sufficiently understood to put into words. She has outgrown him.

They turn into a lane sheltered by hawthorn hedges in full flower. Perhaps merely so as to change the subject, he asks her, "What are you planning to do when the war is over?"

Her thoughts fly to her parents and shy away: the subject is taboo for her.

How can she plan? she asks back. She doesn't even yet know if she is going to be allowed to remain in England. How come? KV asks. Her husband is in the British Army! In *his* army, he explains, a foreigner acquires American citizenship after three months.

Like her parents' failure to leave Germany, the British attitude to refugees is something she prefers not to discuss with him; she is too unsure of her self-control. She says something about finding another husband. She is not referring to Kurt; she knows that he will not marry her. But whether or not her parents survive the war, by now she is old enough to want a home of her own. She wants to have children; Tom has told her that becoming a mother is a requisite step to becoming a whole woman. She belongs to a generation of girls who still see their role in life as secondary to that of some man, a generation in which girls don't expect to have careers unless they happen to have a vocation. Kate has a vocation to make poems but that, she knows, will not earn her a living.

"A girl like you should study," KV says.

That it isn't too late for her to do that comes to her as a totally new idea; no one, not even Tom, who is after all himself a student, has ever suggested it. She had left school in Germany before her fifteenth birthday. Since before then she had been preparing herself for kibbutz life and after giving up that idea she has needed to earn her living. "You could go to night-school," KV says. But already, she doesn't need him to illuminate the way for her; he has acted as her signpost and now she has passed it. As an American, he is ignorant of conditions in Great Britain; she knows that Tom is the one who will give her the information she needs.

When, later in the week, she tells Mrs. Waley of her decision to go to university, and admits that what gave her the idea was a conversation with KV, Mrs. Waley exclaims, "But that is like a skylark being influenced by . . . I don't know what . . . a blackbird!"

Her experiences as a Jew under the Nazis, as a refugee in wartime Britain, have conditioned her to think of herself as an inferior human being, permanently relegated to a second-class life. By wanting to become a university student she is perhaps aiming beyond her reach?

In an idle moment, in Mrs. Waley's sitting-room, she opens a volume of *Shakespeare's Complete Works* as the pious consult the

Bible. It offers her this passage from *Measure for Measure:* "Our doubts are traitors, / And make us lose the good we oft might win, / By fearing to attempt."

Because of the rumours concerning the fate of the Jews on the continent, which had begun to circulate even before Anne's death, and to which I was not always quick enough to close my ears, I did not, as other people did, look forward to the time when the war would be over. But for the last eleven months of its duration I was content: my life had acquired a problem which it was within my powers to solve.

Tom talked me out of trying for Oxford or Cambridge, because there I would face the additional discrimination against females. He and his brother had been brought to Edinburgh by their father because of the reputation of its medical school. He knew nothing about the other faculties, he told me, but was willing to enquire on my behalf. Which one did I want to study in? he asked, with a faith in the adequacy of my intelligence for which I almost loved him. The question opened vistas but could have only one answer: what I was reaching for was proof that as far as the English language was concerned, I was the equal of those who had been born to it.

Although I was writing—I was unable to stop doing it—I did not talk about it in those days when I was not producing anything fit to be shown, anything by which I would have wanted my ability to be judged. I had never mentioned it at Miss Johnson's, knowing what the response would have been; it was echoed round the tea-table by the consensus of opinion that I ought not to study, among native English-speakers, for a degree in English.

"Think how easy it would be for you to get a first-class degree in German," Miss Johnson said. But that would have done nothing to make me feel better about being who I was. Nor would taking up Mr. Ian's suggestion to qualify as an accountant; he spoke of me to some of his business friends, who agreed to join him in financing my studies on the understanding that I would afterwards work for them.

I didn't need to decide yet what subjects I wanted to study, Tom assured me: first I needed to pass the Preliminary Examination, equivalent to the exams taken by school-leavers. I would not have known how to set about finding out what the requirements were. I would perhaps not have wanted to find out: the euphoria of having set myself an aim which was achievable within the foreseeable future was soon countermanded by my usual self-doubts. But I felt committed, too embarrassed to withdraw, once Tom had taken the trouble to procure for me a handful of old examination papers in the subjects in which I would need to pass before I could enter the Faculty of Arts. Encouraged by him and Shakespeare, I went on behaving as if I believed in myself.

I was making my plans at the time of the Allied landings in Normandy, when no one could know for how much longer the war would last. My twenty-first birthday was coming up: I had already passed the age at which people normally enrolled at university. But the reason why I felt myself to be so driven was, I think, the subliminal realisation that I needed to get a hold on a bit of the future to help me across the change-over from wartime to peace, which, for me, would mean being confronted with the fate of my parents. Though I believed that I was impatient because I had already wasted all these years.

Preliminary Examinations were held in September and March. I decided to take the ones in German and in English that autumn, and the ones in French and mathematics the following spring, so that I would be able to start at the university in the autumn of 1945. There was also a scholarship examination, held in May. Once I knew about it I decided to compete; I needed an additional subject for it and chose Medieval English History. I knew more about modern European history but felt that I could not cope, emotionally, with the period which included the First World War, in which my father had fought beside those who were now his enemies against those who had saved me from the concentration camps.

I needed to reach the Higher Standard in all except math; but this subject was compulsory and even the Lower Standard included algebra and some geometry and even trigonometry, for which I needed a teacher, as I did for French. Tom recommended Esther Wallach, who was coaching his brother in Latin. She was Jewish, not much older than I, and earned her living giving private tuition. She coached me in French at a discount because, she said, I was so easy to teach. She supplied a retired teacher who coached me in math.

It was not arrogance but humility which made me give myself so little time to prepare for the examinations: providing me beforehand with an excuse for failing them. No one was more surprised than myself when I passed them all. I came forty-third on the scholarship list; I wished that it had not been published in the *Scotsman,* where Mr. Ian saw it. I was so ashamed. But he and everyone else thought that I had done splendidly, competing against youngsters from all over Scotland who, according to Esther Wallach, had stayed on at school for an extra year to prepare themselves for it. Like Mr. Ian, she spoke of me to her friends, one of whom offered to finance my studies, unconditionally. There was no need: the Refugee Students' Aid Committee in Scotland awarded me a grant.

For the last eleven months of the war, every evening on leaving the shop, if I was not due for a lesson, I was confronted with the choice of remaining among people by going to the cinema, which I so loved doing; often I wandered about, going first in one direction and then in another, unable to make up my mind to go home and study as I knew I ought to do, because no one was waiting there for me and I would be alone. At the entrance to the cinema I would turn away; on the fringe of The Meadows I would turn back again. It was a sweet relief to surrender to my craving; but then I would sit through the film with a nagging conscience, and if it was one I had seen before, or one I had gone to because I had heard it praised by others and it wasn't to my taste, I would leave in the middle of the programme, to get back to my studies.

After Anne's death, I had started to read books on philosophy, on religion, on psychology, and discovered that, instead of numbing my sensibility with fiction, I could also numb it with thought. Now, whenever reality became more than I could bear, so as not to waste my time altogether I resorted to reading novels in French. I felt better about being who I was during an evening spent studying: it made me feel that I had reason to approve of myself. To generate this feeling after an evening spent at the cinema, I would afterwards stay awake reading far into the night.

I did not much want to go to sleep because it meant waking up again. An early night made no difference to my constant headaches. Being without a headache made no real difference to the awfulness of waking up to be me. Even the prospect of becoming a university student could not stop me from hating my life, and myself, and especially my body as if it were not an integral part of me. My childhood dissatisfaction with it had been increased to loathing, first by Walter, because it still pleased him when he could no longer please me, and then by Kurt, since it prevented him from being able fully to reciprocate my love. It caused me to lead an unhealthy life. And I got satisfaction out of doing so: because it proved that my parents ought not to have sent me away.

Although we were all "girls" to Mr. Ian, when he wanted to speak to us he sought us out; so that when, one day late in April, I was told that he wanted to see me in his office, I ran down expecting something good to come of this summons: a small gift of food, a complimentary ticket to a show—something like that. He told me that the Red Cross had published lists of the names of those who had survived the concentration camps; there were copies of them in an office along the road; he told me the house number.

"Thank you very much for telling me," I said: I would go along in my lunch-hour.

He looked at me as if he doubted that I had understood him. If I wanted to go straight away, he suggested, that would be all right. Did I want to take someone with me, Margaret perhaps?

I would have liked to have gone with him, who for almost three years had been the lightning conductor for my filial feelings; I did not think that I could ask it of him. I said that I would prefer to go by myself.

I did not even take my apron off, perhaps so as not to make too much of the occasion. The sun was shining, there wasn't a cloud in the sky; George Street was always quiet, there were no more than two or three people about. I found the house; pinned to the jamb of the open door was a notice in red ink, the words underlined with an arrow pointing up narrow dark uncovered stairs. Off the second half-landing, up one step, the door standing open, was a small room with nothing at all in it except a plain wooden table, stained dark, on which the lists were lying. They were stapled-together small-sized pieces of flimsy paper closely covered in typescript with names, each with a date of birth and a place of residence before deportation, in alphabetical order, grouped according to regions.

I found the list headed Westfalen (Westphalia); it consisted of only one page. I looked down it; there was not even a name beginning with *L.*

I had done what I had come to do so quickly that I went on looking, idly, just for something to do: to provide myself with an excuse for going on standing there while I thought about what I had *not* found out. I had *not* found out that my parents, or my father, or my mother had survived. What I had also not found out was that they had *not* survived. What I had failed to find out did not mean that they were dead.

But I wanted them to be that; that was why I had not been eager to look at the lists. The British had entered Belsen the week before, the Russians had come upon the most easterly of the concentration camps already the previous summer. I would not have wanted to go on living after experiencing what my parents must have experienced. Without having experienced it, merely knowing, or not yet even knowing but surmising what human beings were capable of doing one to another made me want no longer to be alive.

As long ago as after Anne's death I had said, at Miss Johnson's and to Margaret, that I hoped that my parents would not survive the war so that I would not need to tell them that Anne was dead, but I had not meant it, had gone on depositing my soldier's wife's allowance in my savings account, which was the only preparation it was possible for me to make against the day when I would be able to set out to return to them.

I have forgotten just when Walter, with the British Army, passed through Bielefeld; it must have been sometime in May. He spoke with Jewish survivors who had been deported together with my parents to the Riga ghetto in December 1941. He was told that the Jews there worked as slaves for the *Wehrmacht* and that my father, after a year or so, was one morning found dead in his bed—he had a weak heart—and that my mother was known to have survived until the autumn of 1944, when the Germans put an end to the ghetto. No one could tell him what had happened to her.

I did not mourn my parents—then. I had been living as an orphan for so long that it was easy for me to deceive myself into believing that their death made no real difference to me. Their sending me to safety had *felt* to me like a rejection. What had been done to them I could at first cope with only by thinking that they must have deserved it.

The Jews must be a terrible people, I thought, for the rest of the world throughout the ages to have hated them so—blaming for our persecution not the perpetrators but the victims, perhaps because this allowed me to believe that we ourselves were able to do something about it. Not understanding that the reaction of Christian peoples to those who did not share their belief and their way of life had always been either to convert or to kill. Not understanding that the laws of the lands in which we found ourselves were responsible for what we became: bankers to kings in most of Europe, and peddlers in Poland. Not understanding that rulers need scapegoats. And a cause *against* which to unite their subjects. That individuals need to farm out their devils. That once the precedent existed the Jews were the easiest and most obvious target. That I knew Jews from the inside as I did not know other people, and that the faults I could see in them were part of being human.

At the time when I had left my parents, I had been, emotionally, in rebellion against my mother, and did not know that this was normal for an adolescent. At the time I blamed her and later I blamed myself. And because our separation was meant to be temporary but was permanent, my feelings for her, against her, remained frozen at that stage. And because later I had no one who had known her better than I, I know of her only what I remember, know how I saw her and not what she was like.

I remember how I saw my father but don't know what he was like. At the time of our separation I adored him. But because I had witnessed, suffered the consequences of his inability to provide for his family, to protect himself and us from persecution, I thought him incompetent, weak; I could adore him—as I needed to do as an adolescent—only by seeing myself as inferior even to him.

And because I did not see myself—rightly, I still think—as the equal of my parents, and because I believed that they must somehow have deserved their fate, I believed that I deserved at least to have shared it. Perhaps that was what prevented me, for years, from informing myself about it; but I needed that information before I could understand the events of the Holocaust—to the extent to which it is possible to understand them. I needed that understanding before I could accept my Jewishness, and without doing this I could not accept myself.

I have always been tempted by suicide, that ultimate assertion that we and we alone are in charge of our lives. Looking back, it astonishes me that I did not attempt it then. Probably because I saw myself as the keeper of my mother's and my father's and my sister Anne's memory. Lise's existence I ignored because she had left me.

The momentum of my year-long preparation carried me through my first term at the university before I dropped out. As has happened to me with so many experiences, being a student was not as I had imagined it. Getting an honour's degree in French, which was what I had allowed myself to be persuaded to aim for, was altogether irrelevant to what I wanted to do with this life which my parents and the British people had preserved for me: to begin another family—which I did—and to write—which I continue to do.

St. Austell, April 1992

Poet and writer Karen Gershon (1923–93) was born Kaethe Loewenthal in the German province of Westphalia. She was sent to England on a *Kindertransport* in 1938. Ten years later she married a Gentile art teacher, Val Tripp. They had four children. In 1957, she assumed the nom de plume Karen Gershon, her father's Hebrew name, meaning "stranger in a strange land." The Tripps emigrated to Israel in 1968, returning to Britain in 1973.

Phyllis Lassner is a professor at Northwestern University, teaching courses in writing, Jewish studies, and gender studies. She is the author of two books on Elizabeth Bowen; *British Women Writers of World War II; Colonial Strangers: Women Writing the End of the British Empire;* and, in addition to articles on interwar and wartime women writers, *Anglo-Jewish Women Writing the Holocaust.*

Peter Lawson is an associate lecturer at the Open University in London. He is the author of *Anglo-Jewish Poetry from Isaac Rosenberg to Elaine Feinstein* and the editor of a unique anthology of poems, *Passionate Renewal: Jewish Poetry in Britain Since 1945*. He has written widely on Holocaust literature, including *Kindertransport* poetry.

Jewish Lives

For a complete list of titles, see the Northwestern University Press Web site at www.nupress.northwestern.edu.

THOMAS TOIVI BLATT
From the Ashes of Sobibor: A Story of Survival

VICTOR ERLICH
Child of a Turbulent Century

IDA FINK
A Scrap of Time and Other Stories

LALA FISHMAN AND STEVEN WEINGARTNER
Lala's Story: A Memoir of the Holocaust

LISA FITTKO
Escape Through the Pyrenees
Solidarity and Treason: Resistance and Exile, 1933–1940

HANS FRANKENTHAL
The Unwelcome One: Returning Home from Auschwitz

KAREN GERSHON
A Tempered Wind: An Autobiography

RICHARD GLAZAR
Trap with a Green Fence: Survival in Treblinka

MICHAŁ GŁOWIŃSKI
The Black Seasons

HENRYK GRYNBERG
Children of Zion
The Jewish War *and* The Victory

JAKUB GUTENBAUM AND AGNIESZKA LATAŁA, EDS.
The Last Eyewitnesses: Children of the Holocaust Speak (volume 2)

INGEBORG HECHT
Invisible Walls *and* To Remember Is to Heal

Jost Hermand
A Hitler Youth in Poland: The Nazis' Program for Evacuating Children During World War II

Gertrud Kolmar
My Gaze Is Turned Inward: Letters, 1934–1943

Arnošt Lustig
The Bitter Smell of Almonds: Selected Fiction
Children of the Holocaust
The House of Returned Echoes
The Unloved: From the Diary of Perla S.

Liana Millu
Smoke over Birkenau

Thomas Nolden and Frances Malino, Eds.
Voices of the Diaspora: Jewish Women Writing in Contemporary Europe

Bernhard Press
The Murder of the Jews in Latvia, 1941–1945

Wiktoria Śliwowska, Ed.
The Last Eyewitnesses: Children of the Holocaust Speak (volume 1)

Isaiah Spiegel
Ghetto Kingdom: Tales of the Łódź Ghetto

Jiří Weil
Life with a Star
Mendelssohn Is on the Roof

Joanna Wiszniewicz
And Yet I Still Have Dreams: A Story of a Certain Loneliness